PRAISE FOR

"This is an age when are often bandied about with no idea what they really mean. In *The Namaste Effect*, Nischala Joy Devi takes us deep into the true heart of these spiritual treasures. With her own profound understanding, she opens doors and leads us into the real spiritual meaning, showing us how to use it to enhance our inner lives, our lives in the world, and our hearts."

—Prakasha Shakti Capen, Spiritual Teacher, Integral Yoga Minister

"I've always believed the heart is the final destination of all spiritual traditions, including the chakras. This wonderful book, written through the lens of the chakra system, simply shines with love on every page, with an engaging style that makes you feel you are in the arms of a loving mother reading you a story at bedtime. Yet hidden with these pages is a treasure trove of deep spiritual wisdom."

—Anodea Judith, author of *Wheels of Life*, *The Global Heart Awakens*, and *Eastern Body, Western Mind*

"Nischala Devi's book is a journey we must all someday take to understand our most hidden desires and our need for love and happiness. Through the vehicle of the 7 Mystical Chakras, this wise and compassionate teacher shows us how we can truly 'light up the world' and become agents for positive change on this planet."

—Nischala Cryer, co-founder, Ananda University, author of *The Four Stages of Yoga*

"*The Namaste Effect* is brilliant. Nischala Joy Devi, a masterful guide and educator, comes from a deep place of love and oneness, inspiring us to do the same. *The Namaste Effect* illuminates each of the major chakras with a heartfelt and loving touch that rings with truth. She brings each chakra to life with soul, science, storytelling, and especially with love. *The Namaste Effect* sings and soars with insights galore. Nischala draws from a plethora of cultural, religious, literary and sacred traditions to illuminate these valuable teachings for practical and spiritual living. The information, affirmations and meditations offered will illuminate and inspire you on your path of self-understanding and right action, empowered with love and devotion Its uplifting message of peace, love, and acceptance of oneself and others is sorely needed in today's world. This book thoroughly beams brightly. I urge you to get a copy to find out for yourself."

—Julie Lusk, MEd, E-RYT 500, author of Yoga Nidra for Complete Relaxation and Stress Relief

"*The Namaste Effect* is a heart-opening call to an inner awakening for a loving and compassionate life. Nischala Devi relates the subject of the chakras to an open spirituality which draws from religious and philosophical thoughts both from the East and the West. Each chakra is presented with its element, sensory scope, psychology and transformative spiritual power. The reader is uplifted by many real life stories which show that a positive personal change is possible. The examples from Nischala Devi's own life reveal her passion to heal the human heart with Love. May this book open many gates of spiritual understanding and inner learning."

—Swami Durgananda, director, Sivananda Yoga Vedanta Centers Europe

"We need this book now! Each Chakra has a chapter with teaching stories, profound wisdom and practices drawn from Nischala Devi's long years on the path, from devotee to her ground-breaking work with the Dean Ornish program, to a place of spiritual leadership in the world. Reading *The Namaste Effect* is like sitting at the feet of a master story-teller and teacher who is helping us learn, practice and grow into unconditional love."

—Amy Weintraub, Founder of LifeForce Yoga, author of *Yoga for Depression*, *Yoga Skills for Therapists* and the forthcoming, *Temple Dancer*

"Nischala Devi is simply a beautiful being I am honored to call my friend. Let her be your guide on this sacred path towards love, compassionate and genuine caring."

—Deva Premal, Mantra singer, Spiritual Musician and Composer

The Namaste Effect

Expressing Universal Love Through the Chakras

Nischala Joy Devi

Lotus Flower Books

Also by Nischala Joy Devi
The Healing Path of Yoga
The Secret Power of Yoga

The Namaste Effect
Published by Lotus Flower Books, an imprint of
Columbine Publishing Group LLC
PO Box 416, Angel Fire, NM 87710
columbinepublishinggroup.com

Copyright © 2019 Nischala Joy Devi
All rights reserved. No part of this book may be reproduced or transmitted in any form or by any means, electronic or mechanical, including photocopying, recording, or by an information storage and retrieval system without permission in writing from the publisher.

Book layout and design by Lotus Flower Books

First trade paperback edition: May, 2019
First e-book editions: May, 2019

Publisher's Cataloging-in-Publication Data

Devi, Nischala Joy.
The namaste effect : expressing universal love through the chakras / Nischala Joy Devi. — 1st edition
1. Yoga. 2. Spiritual practice. 3. Chakras. I. Title.

ISBN 978-1945422652 trade paperback
ISBN 978-1945422669 e-book

*To all those that embrace the eternal source
of love and oneness*

Contents

Exploring The Namaste Effect	13
The Seven Mystical Chakras	31

Chapter 1 - Muladhara Chakra   45
Survival and Connection
When I am in the place of love and oneness,
I am one with Mother Earth.

Chapter 2 - Swadhisthana Chakra   75
Creativity and Relationships
When I am in the place of love and oneness,
I am creative and embrace loving relationships.

Chapter 3 - Manipura Chakra   105
The Power and the Intellect
When I am in the place of love and oneness,
I am empowered and empower others.

Chapter 4 - Anahatha Chakra   141
Love and Compassion
When I am in the place of love and oneness,
I feel compassion and love for all.

Chapter 5 - Vishudda Chakra   175
Understanding and Higher Communication
When I am in the place of love and oneness,
I understand everything.

Chapter 6 - Ajna Chakra 209
Wisdom and Knowledge
When I am in the place of love and oneness,
I know everything.

Chapter 7 - Sahasara Chakra 239
Oneness
When I am in the place of love and oneness,
I am one with everything.

Continuing Namaste 267

A Grateful Namaste 274

Namaste

"I honor the place within you where the
entire Universe resides;
I honor the place within you of love, of light,
of truth, of peace;
I honor the place within you, where,
when you are in that place in you,
and I am in that place in me,
there is only one of us."
—Mahatma Gandhi

Exploring the Namaste Effect

Namaste, When I am in the place of love and oneness and you are in the place of love and oneness, we are one, Namaste.

A Spoonful of Compassion

"Don't tell me you have been in with a patient, simply listening to her talk and comforting her when she cried. That is a waste of time. Keep that up and I will have to dismiss you from this training program."

This was the response from my supervisor after I was summoned, failing to report exactly on time after performing a procedure in a patient's room.

Systematically working through the list of patients for that morning's rounds at the hospital, I had confidently walked into the room of a young woman with terminal cancer. Six months pregnant with three young children at home, she appeared very frightened and hopeless. I was there to do some procedure, can't even remember what it was. Starting to take out the instruments, I glanced up and our eyes met. At that moment, I could feel a shift in my heart that transformed the room.

Placing the instruments on the bedside table, I enacted what my heart dictated. Tenderly edging myself into the hospital bed, I gently embraced her. Almost simultaneously, she moved toward and encircled me with her arms. Embracing each other, we wept.

Breaking the spell, the crackling loud speaker called my name. Coming back to mental consciousness, I excused myself and walked toward what I knew would be a scolding for obeying my heart rather than hospital rules.

After so many years, my reflection of the events still holds sway. Accused of wasting time with the sweet young mother with cancer became a turning point, and was an everlasting example for me of two hearts recognizing each other as one. It was the aspect of oneness that, in its depth, soothes as it heals, not only the patient, but also the and emotions react. When enriched and refined through reading, education and observation, we are able to utilize the power and potential that a sharp intellect and mind grants.

Keeping the body and mind well-tuned and alert serves us in our present and future situations. But how many of us are really conscious of the role our hearts play in our lives? Do we truly understand what they need to feel supported enough to open? Perhaps during times of great pain *or* effervescent joy we get a glimpse of the heart's purpose in our lives.

It is in the stable moments between the highs and lows that we are able to tap into the unlimited source of love. Those precious pauses reveal our abundant capacity to cherish one another. We remember that the same Divine essence abides in everyone, and that knowledge uplifts and sustains us when equanimity is a distant quality.

We enter into this world openhearted and loving. Eyes wide open, we accept everyone as an aspect of the Divine Self. Welcoming all into our hearts, we smile. It is difficult to resist the purity and love of a newborn. From their innocent way of loving, we are reminded of the purity of our own hearts. As our view of the world and our mental capacity develop, our hearts seem to take a back seat to the mental chatter which demands center stage. As time goes on we learn to analyze, discern and discriminate. Before long, the memory of the oneness inherent in our hearts becomes shrouded by the judging mind. The hope of oneness is a vision of the past.

Why do we become stingy with that love? What would cause us to keep this precious gem hidden? Could fear, anxiety, distrust, even anger be more our nature than loving? Does the innocence of love stay with childhood? Why are we busy building walls to protect our hearts? In our attempt to keep the love in, we are actually keeping love OUT!

We seem to have a fear of sharing our hearts. But why? Could that love hold the power to heal strife with friends, family, governments, countries, and our Mother Earth? Could healing it be as simple as loving others and recognizing that we are one?

Namaste, When I am in that place of love and oneness and you are in that place of love and oneness, we are one, Namaste.

Can Love Be Impersonal?

Most of the time, the way we act and speak of love shows us that our expression of love is conditional. My neighbor built a high fence, they leave their garbage out at night; why should I waste my love on people like that? My father will not give me permission to go on a motorbike; I will withhold my love from him. On and on, we lament how unfairly we are treated and keep that most precious commodity we have, our love, veiled.

What would be the occasion to unleash that shrouded love and compassion? When faced with crises—be they floods, storms, power outages, even attacks on one's country—we cleave together for help and support. We cast aside our differences. Our hearts, bearing compassion, loom forward to overtake the preconceptions, the likes and dislikes, and we experience love. At other times that love and caring seems to be stored deep within, lying dormant, waiting for a crisis to blossom.

After the heinous events of September 11, 2001, parents were at a loss for what to tell their small children. If they vilified the actions of a few, would the impressionable minds and hearts always feel maligned with the groups rebuked?

Seeking the advice of a modern-day sage, Mister Rogers, they were given the key to soothing a shattered heart. "Tell them to watch the helpers." In that way, we are inspired instead of denigrated. Watching people just like us, helping others in need, uplifts us. Sublimating their fear and fury, prejudices and anger to offer love and compassion regardless of their skill level, honors the entire world.

What would the world be like if we realized we needed to express love as much as we need to breathe? Imagine that each time we inhaled, unfiltered love rushed in and satiated each cell. And each time we exhaled, we sent love from our hearts out to the world.

In our desire to function independently, efficiently, and spark our competitive nature, we have estranged ourselves from our divine nature, each other and our Mother Earth. When we are able to open to love itself, we become aware of the need for healing. Love has the power to bring us back to wholeness.

Namaste, When I am in the place of love and oneness and you are in the place of love and oneness, we are one, Namaste.

We Are One?

We are one. This is a wonderful phase that is often used to denote unity and comradery, and it tells a great truth. Yet, when we look closely isn't it really a contradiction? "We" is plural, denoting more than one. "One" indicates a single thing or unit, not two or more. How then can we correctly say, "We are one"? For this great truth, we must look beyond English grammar to that place of truth we hold deep within our hearts, the place that resonates no matter how separate we might appear, no matter how different we may feel, embracing the truth that WE, two or more, can in fact be ONE.

Symbolic Meanings in Global Culture

The word and gesture, *Namaste*, expresses respect to all we meet. It is a typical greeting in India, Sri Lanka, Nepal, and throughout most of Southeast Asia, honored by Hindus, Sikhs, Jains, and Buddhists alike. *Namaste* is an expression and gesture used in everyday life. It is an affirmation of spiritual oneness, acknowledging a shared divinity within each of us.

The physical posturing (or mudra) for *Namaste* is reminiscent of the placement of the hands during prayer. It is a poignant symbol made by aligning the five fingers of the right hand with the five fingers of the left hand. Symbolically, the gesture of joining both hands expresses oneness.

In many traditions, each of the hands are relegated to various meanings and duties. Often, the right hand represents masculine qualities of reason and intellect, which draws forth the power of the sun. Conversely, the left hand represents the feminine qualities of intuition, emotion, the power of the moon, and represents mundane or worldly duties.

By uniting the two, the person offering *Namaste* rises above her differences with others and identifies herself with the spiritual aspect of the person she greets. The modest gesture emits an aura of love, respect, and oneness. In the simplest of terms, it is accepted as a humble greeting straight from the heart, and is reciprocated accordingly. The gesture can also be accompanied with or without the spoken word. When we bring the right and left hand together in a gesture of oneness at the heart center, we act, live, and experience the whole world as love.

A Faux Pas

Sometimes, in our effort to stay with our cultural nuances, we are shocked when those less familiar with them stumble in etiquette.

On one of my early trips to India, I was unaccustomed to eating with one hand, as is their custom. I had been schooled on the cultural necessity of using *only* the right hand, as in the Indian tradition each hand has its designated duty.

The right hand is for eating, offering items to others, edible or not, basically any "clean" duty is reserved for this hand. The left hand's duties, however, are less attractive, designated to be the official wiper of "unclean" areas, including after toileting. It is easy to understand how basic hygiene becomes involved in such a segregation.

My major *faux pas* came while struggling to eat a chapatti

(Indian flat bread). Using only the right hand, I could not seem to tear it into bite-sized pieces. Looking around to see if anyone was watching, my left hand cautiously rose and joined in for the wrestling match. Once the chapatti was tackled and divided, the left hand retreated back to its idleness.

Feeling relieved to have successfully completed the clandestine task, I heard an audible gasp from my host and hostess. Flushing a bright crimson, I apologized and verified. "Please remind me, only the right hand is the clean hand, used for higher duties, the left is relegated to the dirty jobs." Heads bobbing, my hosts agreed.

"Please forgive me," I said. Bringing both hands together in a gesture of oneness, I repeated, *Namaste*. The subtle humor was not lost on any of us as we realized both hands are elevated when joined together.

Namaste, When I am in the place of love and oneness
and you are in the place of love and oneness
we are one, Namaste.

In recent times, yoga students and spiritual aspirants all over the world have embraced the term, *Namaste*. Its symbolic greeting contrasts with those imposed in the west where offering and shaking of the hand is reminiscent of the days when we needed assurance that the offered hand was void of any weapon. The military salute looms from the knight in shining armor lifting his visor to expose his eyes, showing trust, if not always friendship.

The often-humble bowing in Japan and China exposes the neck, in the hope that the gesture will be rewarded with friendship, allowing the head to remain firmly on the neck that is being bared.

Once reserved for close family and friends, a growing number of people from countries both east and west are embracing and reviving the hug as a greeting in all its various forms. My personal favorite is when the left sides of the body embrace, heart to heart and they beat as one. The tingling feeling generated while hugging can be long lasting and, with a simple remembrance, can be recalled.

A single heart cell was taken from the heart of one person. It continued to beat as an individual cell, representing the whole heart. It made the sound "blip blop." Another single cell was taken from a different person's heart. It made the sound "blooop blip."

In a laboratory-controlled situation, each of these cells was placed in an individual petri dish. They continued to beat as before. "Blip blop." "Blooop blip." The dishes were moved close together, as one of the cells was carefully transferred to the other's dish. At the very instant the two cells, foreign to each other, touched they ceased to beat. At the very next instant, they started to beat in unison to a totally different rhythm. "Bliiip blooop. Bliiip blooop." The two cells now danced to the same rhythm. When our heart touches another, like the members of a well-tuned orchestra, they beat as one.

Namaste recognizes that duality has existed from millennia, causing separation, strife, and even violence. *Namaste Effect* suggests a way to bring two opposing forces together, ultimately leading to a state of Oneness. The gesture recognizes equality in all and honors the sacredness inherent in all beings.

Story Telling

Throughout our journey toward love and oneness, stories inspire us. They reveal how others overcome hardships, allowing us to identify similar situations in our own lives. This inspires us toward living with an open heart.

As early as we can recall, we have had stories to hearten us. Some were meant to encourage sweet dreams, others to teach us the moral ways of the world. Stories can embolden us to be the best we can be as well as warn us of subtle or definitive threats. Stories seem to be the easiest way to learn and recall lessons without having to experience them personally.

One of the ways I offer the wisdom in this book will be through the telling of stories. Most of them are from real people whose stories offer remedies for healing the traumas and crises in their lives. Some are a composite, a few are parables. All are expressions of brave people who chose to take the path of love. They tread this noble path, rather than prolonging the pain and suffering other paths often create.

With fingertip availability to guidance and self-help in today's world, we are able to gather effective tools to deal with ordinary experiences. These tools help us to cope with stressful situations and the disgruntled people who engulf us daily. But do we have the coping skills to quell extraordinary situations that present themselves when least expected?

Did you ever find yourself in a situation that was way beyond your everyday abilities? The tools you normally used became inadequate for the job at hand? Are you able to draw from a place deep inside that radiates strength, even faith? A place that not only allows us to move gracefully through these experiences but allows us to thrive and come out stronger?

What if there are people surrounding you in a subway station who clearly intend you harm? Could you keep your wits about you if you were in a hostile country, about to be taken to an army installation? Seems radical? *The Namaste Effect* brings you stories from people who were tested beyond their limits, and survived by reaching into the depth of their hearts to remember the spirit in everyone. They transformed profound wisdom by creating ways to resolve the traumas that life brings, as their hearts remained open.

Take the time to find your own narrative within their stories. Find out how you can use these stories and beliefs to gratify your life with the joy that is your birthright.

When asked if she thought Lord Jesus ever tested her beyond her limits, Mother Teresa quipped, "No, I do not believe Jesus tests me beyond my limits, I just wish He did not have such a *high opinion* of me!!!"

> "The shortest distance between a human being and truth is a story."
> —Anthony De Mello

Exploring the Namaste Effect

The Namaste Effect explores the mystical *Chakras* in their ability to unleash oneness and unconditional love. The chakras are whirling vortexes connected through subtle channels, which allow cosmic energy to flow up and down our spines. Within its varied attributes, each *chakra* is permeated with the ever-present essence of Love for All.

One of the ways to keep our attention focused on

Universal Love, while reading *The Namaste Effect*, is to have the definition of *Namaste* that relates to the particular chakra constantly reinforced. At various junctures through the text, I have interjected the *Namaste* phrase pertaining to each chakra. For example, while exploring the chapter on the *Manipura Chakra* you will encounter *Namaste, When I am in a place of love and oneness, I am one with Mother Earth, Namaste.* Please take a moment to read and reflect on the phrase. Take a deep breath as you read it aloud again before going on. It will help the heart remember what the mind often forgets.

Our journey through *The Namaste Effect* begins with:

The Seven Mystical Chakras, where the basis of the chakra system is explored and explained. Being a very complex subject, the aspect of the chakras we will focus on will be limited to its quality of Universal Love.

Chapter One - Muladhara Chakra -
Survival and Connection

When I am in a place of love and oneness,
I am one with Mother Earth.

The *Muladhara Chakra* reflects the earth element. It gives us a solid base and is a guide to our survival on our Mother Earth.

Chapter Two - Swadhisthana Chakra -
Creativity and Relationships

When I am in the place of love and oneness,
I am creative and embrace loving relationships.

The Swadhisthana Chakra reflects the water element. We are reminded that life ebbs and flows. It guides us in creativity and in our relationships with others.

Chapter Three - Manipura Chakra -
The Power and the Intellect

When I am in the place of love and oneness,
I am empowered and empower others.

The Manipura Chakra reflects the fire element, revealing the Sun as the source of our worldly power. This fire gives rise to our ability to think and reason. It reveals the essence of our real power as benevolent and kind.

Chapter Four - Anahatha Chakra -
Love and Compassion

When I am in the place of love and oneness,
I feel compassion and love for all.

The Anahatha Chakra, representing the air element, is mutable, ever-present. It allows us to remember our essential nature as love and compassion.

Chapter Five - Vishudda Chakra -
Understanding and Higher Communication

When I am in the place of love and oneness,
I understand everything.

The Vishudda Chakra brings forth the element of ether,

rarified and moving us beyond the earth's jurisdiction, to infinity. We are infused with the ability to understand that which the ordinary mind often does not understand.

Chapter Six - Ajna Chakra - Wisdom and Knowledge

When I am in the place of love and oneness,
I know everything.

The *Ajna Chakra* offers us a connection to the heavens. The rarified *Ajna Chakra*, or the eye of wisdom, gives us insight and knowledge beyond the common comprehension, allowing us to know everything.

Chapter Seven - Sahasara Chakra – Oneness

When I am in a place of love and oneness,
I am one with everything.

The *Sahasara Chakra* propels us through the earth's portal to the heavens and beyond. It draws energy from the universe and infuses our being on a continuous basis through the knowledge that we are ONE.

Filling our lives with inspiration brings us to the center of our hearts where we live in love. Our quest to regain the feeling of oneness must carefully be reflected in the actions we take. Sometimes, without premeditation, the experience of contentment and peace renders words irrelevant. It is the same experience we feel when communing with Mother Nature in all her forms.

We are part of the whole body of humanity, yet we tend to live in our own little milieu, surrounded by life's dreams and dramas. To touch and embrace another allows us to feel the rhythm of our own heart.

Our life's journey on this earth commences as an eternal whisper. This essential energy is vast and infinite. Tomes of scripture, poetry and philosophy, try as they might, have only given us the slightest glimmer of what Universal Love can be. At once, when a ray of universal love journeys forth, seeking a home, it finds refuge in the human heart and transforms Divine energy into a human being. We start as love, and it is up to us to continue that faithful current through our lifetime.

As the pages unfurl, my hope is that *The Namaste Effect* reignites your heart to experience boundless love. Within this powerful energy lies the experience of universal love. It is present and available to all you meet in the vastness of this universe.

Namaste, When I am in the place of love and oneness and you are in the place of love and oneness, we are one, Namaste.

The Seven Mystical Chakras

The Cosmic Flute

Imagine a long, empty hollow tube made of bamboo, wood, or metal with round openings at regular intervals. It is not much more than a hollow empty tube. However, the simple shape allows for the passage of vital life force to flow through it. At a prescribed time, with divine orchestration, cosmic energy circulates through the simple tube and it becomes a musical instrument!

Even as the energy is being blown into the flute, it does not make a sound. Apply a little pressure to one of the openings and you begin to hear a melody. The most beautiful melodies are experienced by the people who have the gift to play their instruments.

We have such a flute within us, in our spinal cord. Housed within this great spinal channel are seven mystical vortexes that blend the spiritual, mental, emotional, and physical worlds. The energy centers, or *chakras*, allow various tones and energies to flow through us, enlivening our entire being.

As the energy flows and dances around the spine, it is as if it is being played by a maestro calling forth life and love. Sometimes one note will be played more often and sometimes another. A few may be activated or remain dormant. And so, the symphony of love and life has begun.

> "Life is like a flute —it may have many holes and emptiness, but if you work with it carefully, magical melodies can flow."
> —Anonymous

The Seven Mystical Powers Within

Within us there are whirling vortexes of energy, called *Chakras*. These seven mystical vortexes are connected through subtle channels that allow cosmic energy to flow up and down our spines.

As the universal energy flows from the heavens into our physical, emotional, and intellectual bodies, it polarizes into two parts. The right side becomes the masculine, cognitive energy, and the left side becomes the intuitive, feminine energy. These two channels traverse at various points along the central channel. They are called respectively *Pingala* on the right and *Ida* on the left. *Pingala* represents masculine characteristics and *Ida* feminine. Crisscrossing around the spine, they allow vital information to be transmitted from the chakra to our bodies, minds, and emotions. They encourage us to function as spiritual *and* human beings concurrently.

The chakras can be further delineated into two groups: four at the top of the spinal channel, which are infused with cosmic energy, and three toward the bottom of the spinal channel, infused with earth energy.

The four upper chakras, *Sahasara, Ajna, Vishudda* and *Anahatha*, are known for holding the highest aspects of our existence. They are referred to here as Heaven Chakras, as a way of distinguishing them from the three Earth Chakras, *Manipura, Swadhisthana* and *Muladhara*.

Observing the natural division of the human body, we find a large smooth muscle, the diaphragm, residing at the solar plexus. This large hemi-dome muscle is the physical division between the abdominal cavity and the thoracic or chest cavity. Its positioning is very telling. While it is creating a division in the physical body, it also encourages the subtle energy (*apana-vayu*) emerging at the *Manipura Chakra* (power) below the diaphragm to move in a downward direction. It passes through the *Swadhisthana* (sacral) and *Muladhara* (base) chakras, continuing its flow toward the earth. These three chakras, affected by the pull of the subtle downward moving energy (*apana-vayu*), allow us to remain engaged with the earth and all the worldly needs connected with the earth. For this reason, I have identified these three chakras below the diaphragm as the Earth Chakras. Connecting with this energy force sanctions us to live and function on our planet, Earth.

Starting just slightly below the *Anahatha Chakra*, above the diaphragm, we find an upward moving energy (*prana-vayu*). It presents the counter or reversed function to the *apana-vayu*. The *prana-vayu* ascends through the *Anahatha* (heart), the *Vishudda* (throat) and *Ajna* (third eye) chakras where it then traverses the *Sahasara Chakra*, emerging through the top of the head, allowing it to reunite with the vastness of the Universal Consciousness. Here, the cosmic energy infuses us with the knowledge of our divinity. We become aware of the role of the upward moving energy in these four Heaven Chakras. For most of us it takes a concerted effort to stay connected to the Heaven Chakras, as the world we move in anchors us to the earth and the chakras that represent it.

We find in much of the literature, the most common way of describing this pattern; the Earth Chakras are designated as "lower" while the Heaven Chakras are deemed as "higher." This tends to polarize them even further, implying that the Earth Chakras are somehow not as important as the Heaven Chakras. This thought infers that if our energy vibrates with the Earth, we live and function at a lower level. Holding our deepest aspiration of exhibiting palpable spiritual qualities, we may choose to function *exclusively* through the Heaven Chakras. This is not possible, as we need to function simultaneously with both Earth and Heaven energies. Relying solely on the Heaven Chakras to guide us is not possible as we must maintain our connection with the Earth as long as we are a part of Her. As the Earth Chakras come into balance, they support us to focus awareness on the Heaven Chakras and beyond.

All the chakras are of vital importance and each has a specific function. When the Earth centers are in balance, we feel grounded and steady, able to easily deal with whatever situation may arise. When the Heaven centers are in harmony, we remember our love for all and know we are One in the Spirit. Our hope is to bring about balance in the Earth and Heaven Chakras, enabling us to move with ease through life, being at once human while basking in our spiritual power.

When unencumbered, the energy easily flows; we feel whole, healthy, and experience love for all. As this divine energy propels and evolves, these seven vital vortexes of energy (the *Seven Mystical Chakras*) direct our every feeling, emotion, thought, and action. With the stresses of everyday life, the flow is hindered, causing us to feel lethargic, anxious, depressed or even diseased. When these subtle energy centers are in balance, they resonate with each other and remind us, *we are one with everyone and everything.*

Balancing

We are able to use simple techniques and practices to enhance and balance these mystical centers. With consistency, we experience an equilibrium that impacts our bodies, minds and our entire life, which ultimately affects the world at large.

This mystical system is an aspect of our subtle nervous system. It can not be defined in physical terms, as it abides in the part of us that is elusive. In our day-to-day existence, we may not be aware that we have chakras. We imagine that if they were *real* we could see them, touch them, or at least hear them. In actuality, it is *our* inability to focus our inner perception that does not allow us to discern their existence.

To understand the subtle, we need only to bring the extraordinary perception to the ordinary. Typically, we relegate extraordinary "knowing" to only a few, because it is seemingly out of our common experience. Yet, the capacity to understand the extraordinary is well within our grasp; this ability is determined by where we focus our awareness. Whether we believe in them or not, the chakras infuse each part of us with subtle energy, which can be employed for the ordinary as well as the extraordinary.

Still skeptical? We are not able to see the air we breathe, yet we all agree it is there and we cannot exist without it. We have made an unspoken agreement that, seen or not, it does exist! Can we do the same with the chakras?

If we walk along the street, looking down at the petite flowers growing in the cracks of the pavement, the colorful hot-air balloon floating in the sky may not be seen. Delighting in the novelty of the floating balloon, a friend may try to describe it to us. But we are not able to directly perceive it because we are focused elsewhere. Because we are unable to see it, we doubt its existence.

That same misperception can be applied to the energy centers. If we are unaware of them, we do not have the quest for discovery. Once they are introduced to us, we are able to attune to them. With guidance and tenacity, they can be seen with the third eye or perceived by the other senses as to how they interact with our bodies, minds, and lives. As we are able to experience their radiance and power, we honor their existence and attune to them. They then become tools for transformation.

Whirling Vortexes of Love

The first seers, thousands of years ago, recognized chakras as energy centers. The closest word they could find to describe these indescribable energy centers was the Sanskrit word meaning wheel—*chakra*.

In essence, chakras are much more than wheels. Neither flat nor two dimensional, they have been described as whirling vortexes of energy—similar to the sun. If we glimpse the sun from earth or look at a photo, it appears to be a flat disc. But peer through a telescope to see a close-up of the sun, you'll find that it is constantly pulsating, with energy erupting all around it. It is similar to how the chakras appear within you.

When the spirit takes a physical body, a clear definition is formed between the physical, emotional, and intellectual aspects of our being. *Each* aspect receives nourishment from the chakras.

The seven chakras contain all the information that our souls have gathered throughout our existence in time, similar to the programming of a computer. At first glance, a computer chip doesn't look like much. But when put in place, an enormous amount information is released from that minute chip.

As our journey through the chakras begins, we are instantly awed by the sheer magnitude of information we are able to access.

The chakra system, being esoteric, is difficult to comprehend using only the cognitive mind. I invite you to engage your intuition, to coax the chakras to reveal their secrets.

> "The intuitive mind is a sacred gift and the rational mind is a faithful servant. We have created a society that honors the servant and has forgotten the gift."—Albert Einstein

For the purpose of our discovery, we will identify and codify the chakras in specific ways. Our exploration leads us to discover the natural element each represents, the color with which it vibrates, and the qualities it puts forth that enable us to function on the earth.

Chakras Closed or Open?

Has anyone ever told you, "Your chakra is closed?" In actuality, it is impossible to live with a closed chakra. In our effort to understand a very subtle and esoteric concept, we equate it to a physical assessment, either open or closed. It is our attempt to fathom how this very subtle and clandestine energy functions. If the vibratory energy in one of the whirling vortexes slows, the function of that chakra is hindered. That change manifests in physical, mental, or emotional ways. Whereas, when the energy in the chakra begins to vibrate more rapidly, the energy moves freely. This is more accurate than saying the chakra is "open," often a misleading term. Substituting the words *harmonizing* and *balancing* for the dubious open and closed puts this concept in a positive light.

A chakra may be radiating less energy if physical tension or an emotional imbalance exists within us. When we learn to relax the body, calm the mind, and release disturbing emotions, our chakras naturally align and balance. Learning spiritual practices from a bounty of traditions, known to foster equilibrium and balance, encourages the flow of energy through the chakras.

We Are All Divine Beings

Most of the time, when the chakras are expounded upon or written about, the counting starts from the *Muladhara Chakra* (base), typically called the first chakra. Because of the Muladhara Chakra's connection to the earth, this alludes to the premise that we are first and foremost earthlings or human beings. Our desire increases as we strive to achieve the hallowed state, which we are told historically only a very few reach. We mortals then halfheartedly attempt to raise this energy upward from the base chakra, struggling to claim our divinity and attain immortality. That is a typical way of looking at our incarnation from a western philosophical perspective.

However, from more of an eastern metaphysical perspective, our divinity is guaranteed, as it is the essence of who we are. Our life's mission on planet earth is to integrate that divinity with our humanity. The good news is we do not have to strive toward divinity, we are already divine. It is *our* birthright.

The Seven Chakras

Beginning as cosmic energy, the chakras disseminate this energy to various levels of consciousness. The undifferentiated and expanded energy, still in its condensed state, manifests as the *Sahasara Chakra*, the most subtle energy, establishing itself at the crown of the head. It holds the unwavering impression of our oneness with all.

From the subtle, patterns form and infuse the chakras as they manifest and shape our physical and mental qualities. That is how our different attributes emerge. Our characteristics appear from the subtle energy which manifests physically as DNA, thereby creating each very unique person and personality. Where exactly will that birthmark appear? Will she be intelligent or intuitive? Could it even be responsible for a sour or a sweet disposition? These and a plethora of qualities await orders from within the seven chakras.

As the energy descends to the base and awakens our *Muladhara Chakra*, we are prepared to survive in the material world. In their combined intention, the chakras align in function to give us clues and the accompanying lessons to ascend back into the infinite.

We then begin to discern the chakras the way they were created and, in turn, how we were created, from the crown downward, from the heavens to the earth.

The *Sahasara Chakra* functions as the constant connection to our True Self. At this, the highest level of awareness, the quest for union is foremost. The longing to reunite with our spiritual nature is continually present.

As the energy descends from the Crown, the other chakras are created. We slowly become aware of our physical existence manifesting as the next three chakras, directly fed by the cosmic energy, *Ajna* (brow point), *Vishudda* (throat), and *Anahatha* (heart).

Manipura (solar plexus), *Swadhisthana* (sacral plexus) and *Muladhara* (base) secure us to the earth. The Earth Chakras hold the qualities needed to live with ease on this planet. When the Heaven and Earth Chakras balance, we are in harmony with every aspect of life.

You Are a Rainbow of Colors

Of the many books and theories of chakras, very few agree on their characteristics. While most concur about their existence in the subtle realm, the most dominant chakra within each individual dictates how that individual is perceived by others and how that person sees his or her own self. If one has a dominance in the *Manipura Chakra*, where intellect and power are in play, the world would be observed through that vision. The person might see the need to protect themselves or be constantly on the defensive, perceiving that it is them against the world.

Each of the chakras also vibrates at a certain frequency (different from the other chakras) and emits a particular color.

We can tell the health and balance of a chakra according to the intensity of the color. If the color is muddy, it is an indication that it is not in balance, as it is when the color is clear and vibrant. When imaging the color associated with each chakra, allow it to be vibrant and pure.

When the inner light begins its journey to the earth, it prisms into the full spectrum of color; we then discern distinct colors associated with each chakra.

The first ray descending from the opalescent white

color of the *Sahasara Chakra (crown of the head)* is the ultraviolet/violet of the *Ajna Chakra (brow point)*, the eye of wisdom. Its ultraviolet is undetectable to the human eye and affords us the understanding that the *Ajna Chakra* is still out of our normal range of consciousness. As the energy continues to descend, it emits shorter and thinner vibratory rays, which correspond to the vibrations of the color violet. This auric field of violet light is often "seen" in deep meditation.

The light continues to release various colored rays, infusing and illuminating each of the chakras. Moving from the violet of the *Ajna*, the opalescent white light releases a brilliant blue ray which then vibrates as *Vishudda (throat)*, the chakra of understanding.

The white light continues to descend, emitting a soft green ray that creates the *Anahatha Chakra (heart)*, manifesting love and compassion. This color is reminiscent of when the spring is born. When all the chakras both above and below harmonize, the color green transforms into a vibrant pink, which radiates love and compassion.

As the opalescence continues its journey, it creates the Earth Chakras. At the solar plexus, a brilliant yellow energy infuses the *Manipura (solar plexus)*, the chakra of power. As the vibration purifies, the yellow of the sun takes on a golden hue, increasing its vibrancy.

The orange ray illumines the *Swadhisthana*, the chakra of creativity at the sacral plexus. Being a secondary color, it combines the yellow of the *Manipura* with the red of the *Muladhara* chakras to create orange, while maintaining its own unique character.

The longest and the strongest color wavelength on the spectrum generates the energy of the base or *Muladhara*

Chakra. As it connects us to the earth, it vibrates at a rate which produces the hue or color—red. The presence of infrared, a red color invisible to the human eye, allows the subtle connection with the earth to burrow in.

Divinely Human OR Humanly Divine?

Now that many people, less familiar with Yogic Wisdom, are learning about the chakras, the intricate details have to be explained through a western philosophical lens. That belief supports the understanding that we are earthlings and it is our hope, if we are good, to one day ascend to the heavenly qualities. We will honor the western understanding, as we begin our exploration of the chakras in *The Namaste Effect* at the Earth Center, the *Muladhara Chakra*, and venture upward, ultimately arriving at the *Sahasara (crown) Chakra*.

On your journey through the chakras, please hold in your mind and heart the more elusive understanding that we are born divine. This wisdom assumes that we are granted divinity simply by being born, vibrating at the highest level of consciousness. Embracing this highest consciousness, we become human. In this way, the cosmic energy creates each of the seven chakras, infusing them with Universal Love.

For academic purposes we are isolating each chakra, so we may understand their uniqueness and qualities. In actuality, however, they must be interactive and interdependent to form a fully functioning and complete system. It is similar to a rainbow where each color, while appearing independent, melds into the next color on the spectrum.

Embarking on this journey, we reunite our humanity with our divinity. The knowledge that we are at once human *and* divine becomes a reality.

Chapter One

Muladhara Chakra

When I am in a place of love and oneness

I am one with Mother Earth

Survival and Connection

Love Our Mother

I am feeling comfortable in spite of the walls closing in and tightening my body. I feel safe and secure, in want of nothing. I cherish the closeness to my true divine nature; each moment is saturated with a sense of joy.

Suddenly, a violent eruption seems to come from beyond, threatening to expel me from my quiet solitude. Pulsating, it propels me down a long, constricting tunnel. A harsh light, stealing the darkness from the outside, invades the soft luminescence formerly cocooning me. Indeed, the light draws me to it, as well as the sounds, unlike the steady drum I am accustomed to.

Slipping and sliding, I am thrust out of my sheltered home. A pair of enormous hands catch me as if I were a ball. The next strange sensation is of being inflated. The atmosphere is being forced into my lungs. I am aware that my participation is needed to survive in this new environment I now inhabit.

I am encased in a dough-like form that changes erratically and yet seems to want to move in a controllable form. In these new circumstances, the form I inhabit has ways to communicate that are foreign to me. The necessity to take in food as nourishment is contingent on my ability to eat, a new concept inherent in this physical form. When consumed, the food changes form and appears to then ooze from different orifices with no apparent control. I am no longer one with the body who created me; I have been expelled. I am now separate and independent. I am embodied, yet in another form. Made from the earth and dependent on the earth, I shall live. With my first inhalation, I have made a non-revocable contract with Gaia.

> "The essence of all beings is earth." — Chandogya Upanishad

The Muladhara Chakra

Muladhara Chakra, enshrined at the very base of the spine, resonates with the earth element. Imagine energy flowing down the legs as it burrows into the rich earth, returning to the source. Connecting to the earth, we feel grounded, confident, a sense of belonging. Our bodies are made from the elements of the earth. If we are able to remember the oneness, the solidity of earth affords us the confidence to reach upward, embracing the spirit.

The journey from the loftiness of the heavens to the stability of Mother Earth has begun. Donning the earthly body, we now identify ourselves as *merely* human and relegate Earth as our permanent home. It becomes our place of rejuvenation and pleasure, so much so that we forget we are born of spirit, not *just* a physical body.

If we were to buy or sell the elements and minerals that make up our body's composition, the current value would be about $10.00. As absurd as that sounds, it is the value of the individual components taken from the earth. As our awareness dawns, we understand that it is when the spirit infuses the body with life that it becomes valuable. The body is a delightful vehicle that houses this sacred essence.

> "If one destroys the Temple, the one who lives in that temple is also destroyed."
> —Bhagavad Gita

We have the ability to reach outward from the spirit, into the physical world, through the five senses. They invite the outside world to us through seeing, smelling, tasting, feeling, and hearing. The senses become the vantage point from which we observe the world.

The *Muladhara Chakra,* connecting us to the earth's energy, creates a vortex from which our basic survival manifests. All the earth's bounty is there to nurture us. From our first moment of worldly consciousness, we develop a relationship with Her that lasts until the use for the body is complete. Our body is then returned to its rightful owner, Mother Earth.

*Namaste, When I am in a place of love and oneness,
I am one with Mother Earth, Namaste.*

Black and Red

The energy of the *Muladhara Chakra* radiates a downward force toward the earth and vibrates as two distinct colors—red, being the longest color wavelength, and black, being the absence of color.

The color red, dynamic in its hue and intensity, represents the color of the earth itself. In some cases, the soil may appear as brown which is a mixture of red with yellow added. It sustains us on this planet and is reminiscent of the red river (blood) flowing through our bodies, insuring life and vitality. The red is replicated in the mouth and lips and other visible and non-visible membranes of the body.

Red is used to warn us of danger, as in STOP signs and sirens on emergency vehicles.

Seniors find the color attractive, as the vibrancy infuses them with a degree of vitality often needed as the body slows in the aging process. Adding a touch of red brightens any person, room, or accessory. Often used moderately, large splashes of the color can elicit a flare in the physical, as well as the emotional, aspects of our being.

I remember when my 92-year-old mother refused to take off her red sweater. She wore it to meals, on outings, and even to bed! She loved that sweater. Admittedly, it made her look cheery and brightened both the wearer and the observer.

What she could not see, however, was the rather looming threadbare circle on her back that denoted the sweater's overuse and age. Able to see the back, I was embarrassed, imagining that people would think I cared so little for my mother that I allowed her to wear rags. The truth be told, I had tried in vain multiple times to replace the worn garb. She refused, holding tighter to the sweater.

After months of searching, I was rewarded by finding a similar sweater. One night, entering her room as she slept, I clandestinely switched the two. The dawning of the new day revealed my mother dressed as usual in her new red sweater.

~ ~ ~

The alternate color of the *Muladhara Chakra* is black. Technically, black is not *a* color but the absence of *all* color. If we dig a tunnel deep into the earth, we are rewarded with total darkness. Our attempt at bringing this darkness back to the earth's surface is what we call the "color" black. Anytime we need to feel grounded or a sense of stability, the influence of the color black is present. Our familiarity with black objects that naturally occur is often limited to something burnt after a fire, charcoal pellets, or overcooked food. Difficult to find above the earth's crust, it is nonetheless a popular "color" freely used for clothing and home accessories.

When wearing the color black or adding it to your home, frugality must be used.

You might have noticed that people who live in cities tend to wear black. When questioned, most will tout its ability to hide any dirt or mishaps. It has become fashionable to wear black.

If we delve a bit deeper, comparing it to people living in the countryside, we may find another reason. Farmers and people working directly with the land rarely wear black. Their proximity with the earth on a daily basis gives them a deep connection to the earth. Toiling in the soil promotes a feeling of being grounded and releases the necessity to don black clothing. Cities rarely have enough earth to satisfy the craving, so black becomes an obvious choice.

Teaching a workshop on the chakras in New York City, I gave the lunchtime assignment to find a patch of earth and connect to Her. I knew it would be a challenging assignment, especially in the area of the city where the course was given. Deciding to get some fresh air, I went outside to discover one of the students practicing her assignment right outside the front door. There, a single tree stood surrounded by a one-foot circle of earth encased in a foot-high fence. The diligent student had traversed the fence and was meticulously treading the earth, as she circumambulated the tree. Cities are often a difficult place to commune with Mother Earth.

Would it be a bit easier to commune with nature in the country? I was leading a workshop on the outskirts of a large city in Germany. Known for its wonderful forests, Germany has many notorious hikers and lovers of outdoors and nature. When I suggested they find a tree and hug it, I thought they would be delighted. Instead, my suggestion was met with horrified stares. "You mean you want us to go outside, find a tree and put our arms around it?"

"Yes, that is exactly what I am asking you to do."

We left the classroom and ventured to a large grove of tall trees. Some hung back, thinking I wouldn't notice they were straying from the group. The assignment was to find a tree that attracted you, encircle it with your arms, close enough that your heart and belly came into contact with the trunk and its energy. Approaching the small forest, many checked to make sure no one was watching them make fools of themselves. Some tentatively reached out with their hands, keeping their distance, as if the tree at any moment might explode.

Encouraging them by example, I chose a tree friend and embraced it fully, even pressing my cheek against her bark. Following my lead, more joined in. After a few minutes, assuming the exercise was done, the group started to leave. A nod of encouragement brought them back to the tree. After some time, I noticed friendships with the trees were being made. When the time came to separate, some were visibly sad to leave their plant friends. Back in the classroom the ensuing discussion told the true tale; while many felt uncomfortable and embarrassed, all said they felt calm and balanced from simply hugging a tree!

Black, as viewed by the western world, is also the color of mourning. Yet, it has become a fashion statement worn on all occasions, including weddings and happy events. It wears the tag the "little black dress."

Coco Chanel, an innovative fashion designer of the 20th century, seems to be the one responsible for the "little black dress" phenomenon. Her designs revolutionized women's fashion, as she strove to find a perfect balance between comfort and feminine style.

Her dedicated work was second only to her intimate relationship with her partner. Upon his untimely death, she plunged into depression, unable to work or function for months. Her close friends expressed concern. "Please, it is time to return to society, you are still a young woman with a full life ahead." After much persuasion, she reluctantly agreed to attend a party for a close friend. Having worn mourning clothes since the tragic event, she tried to envision what to wear. Unwilling to relinquish her widow's weeds, she accepted the task of creating a fashionable mourning cocktail dress. The concept of the "little black dress" was born.

When wearing or decorating in black, be vigilant for any signs of approaching depression or sadness. Adding a bit of red can make the melancholy fly away.

Can You Smell That?

Housed within the *Muladhara Chakra* is the sense of smell that both entices and warns us of danger. Also present is the emotion of fear. The sense of smell and the emotion of fear intertwine, one feeding the other. Seeking a sense of belonging to the earth, the *Muladhara Chakra* motivates us to attend to the basics of survival: food, clothing, shelter.

The *Muladhara* is the chakra of instinct. How we view

our survival is both complex and basic. Many of our actions are not deeply thought through, especially when it comes to survival. When this chakra develops, it gives us instinctual warnings from a spectrum of dangers to insure our survival.

As babies begin to propel themselves, adults become more vigilant. Depending on our fear level and patience, we may scoop them up and redirect them. Quelling our apprehensions, we become protectors standing behind the crawler as the tot nears a flight of steps, still allowing for exploration and safety. If we are able to watch and observe without interfering, we observe as she gets closer to the top step, the more cautious she becomes. At a certain stage, the *Muladhara Chakra* issues its survival instinct as she backs away from the treacherous steps.

There are a certain few who continually challenge the instinct of survival. We watch, often agape, at the feats performed by aerial artists pushing the fragile survival instinct to its limits. Ever think of jumping out of a perfectly good airplane to journey above the earth, as if flying? Would you climb to lofty heights, not only testing your endurance but the human need for oxygen? Many do.

When our basic survival needs are met, we are able to expand outward, leaving our controlled place of safety to meet new people, visit exotic places, find new adventures. If we are reticent to venture outward, we should look to our relationship with the *Muladhara Chakra*.

Namaste, When I am in a place of love and oneness, I am one with Mother Earth, Namaste.

Harm-less Foods

In these abundant times, we have a plethora of exotic foods from all over the world to tantalize our sense of taste. Among our choices of what to consume, the contest for healthful or not looms. Also, the great debate of whether to eat only plant-based foods or to include animal-based foods, continues. Health advocates are hard pressed to agree on this.

Having embraced Yoga in its entirety and upholding one of its crowning aspects, Ahimsa (cultivating love and compassion for all), I chose many years ago to be vegetarian. This choice was affirmed during our research with Reversing Heart Disease. The studies on Coronary Artery Disease seem to conclude that eating a diet void of animal products is a good preventive and even curative step. However, wherever your choice leads, it is important to honor the food we eat and the earth, the source of the food.

In the Native American tradition, before an animal is killed, a pact is made with the animal's soul. Prayers are recited. Rituals performed. Nothing of the animal is wasted; all parts are utilized. Some are eaten, others are made into clothing, and some are used for making shelters. Honoring the animal this way gives our hearts a burst of compassion and an experience of comradery with the animal and its spirit.

It seems many people are intrigued or at least curious as to what one chooses to eat and why. The curiosity escalates if one chooses to be a vegetarian.

Having a limited time for lunch, I chose to sit at the counter for quicker service, taking a seat next to a small boy who was happily munching a very large cheeseburger.

I smiled, and a nod validated my arrival. Ordering a veggie burger, I sipped a drink, anticipating my sumptuous lunch. On the arrival of my burger, I layered various condiments on the bun. Curious, the young man craned his neck to inspect my food.

"That does not look like my burger," he said.

"It's different," I said, not wanting to get into a philosophical discussion.

"What is different about it?" he pressed on.

"Yours is ground beef and mine is ground vegetables."

"Why aren't you eating ground beef?" The inquiry continued.

"Since I have a choice, I choose to eat vegetables instead of animals."

"Do you love animals?"

"I do," I said, hoping that would end the conversation and I could return to enjoying my meal.

"Hmmm." He thought for a few moments and said, "I see that you love animals, but … I bet that animals *love you* too!"

Namaste, When I am in a place of love and oneness, I am one with Mother Earth, Namaste.

It is always interesting to notice how, as adults, we retain experiences of childhood and build our lives around those experiences. If, as a child, your parents were late paying the rent or were unable to put enough food on the table, it might leave a deep doubt within you as to your ability to survive. If there was not enough money to buy new clothes and you wore only secondhand clothes, when adulthood dawned you might shy away from secondhand stores, choosing only new clothes. Or you might only buy secondhand clothes, thinking you are to worthy of new clothes.

Continual apprehension tarnishes our mind, as well as the flow of energy. Much of the time it is our past experiences, rather than the actualities, which inform our decisions. Our fears as well as our comforts are continually perpetuated. All these experiences form and are housed in the *Muladhara Chakra*.

Communing With Wo/Man's Best Friend

The sense of smell and memory are also contained in the *Muladhara Chakra*, along with assuring safety or warning of peril. As children, we often identify our parents by the way they smell or by the particular fragrance they wear, a specific type of perfume, cologne, aftershave, shampoo, or even the scent of a particular clothes detergent.

Years later, passing a stranger on the street, we may unexplainably find a feeling of comfort embracing us. Curious why we would feel that from a passerby, our memory recalls our mother wearing that very fragrance. The sense of smell triggers memory, which then relates directly to instinct. Our instinct allows us to react to a variety of situations in a protective way.

This sense of smell, when attributed to animals both wild and domesticated, is much more acute than ours. It enables them to sense friend or foe with their acute sniffers.

I was visiting a friend with a high-spirited dog that was very happy to see me. He bolted excitedly toward me, circling around my back while his nose, at the perfect height and dimension, was inserted in a place that caused me to jump. This kind of a greeting would be considered highly inappropriate in most situations, but coming from a dog it was somewhat more tolerable.

"It is a bad habit," my very embarrassed friend offered as a weak apology.

"As strange as it seems to us, it is more of an instinctive reaction than a bad habit. He is deciding if I smell trustworthy or not."

Our instinct through the sense of smell alerts us to danger, our mind then decides whether to react to it or not. Instinct is a companion to the sense of smell. Have you ever had the opportunity to be near an animal, perhaps a cat or dog, after she has just given birth? The act of birthing itself is instinctual even if it is the first time, imparting vital information on how to care for the young. Birth also triggers the olfactory sense of the newborn kittens and puppies. Initially unable to see, they must use their well-equipped sense of smell to locate their mother's nipples, the key to their survival.

This is also true for human babies. An interesting experiment was done, with ten newborn human babies and their mothers. Offering the mothers an infant other than her own, the women took the newborns to the breast. The babies, even at that tender age, were able to discern that this comforting stranger was not their mother and refused the offer of food. The newborns were again moved to other arms and breasts with the same results. Their survival instinct on alert, the offered nourishment was rejected. When they were once again held safely in their birth mothers' arms, the baby's sense of smell revealed the correct place for the feast.

*Namaste, When I am in a place of love and oneness,
I am one with Mother Earth, Namaste.*

An Accurate Cancer Screening?

There is much research being conducted to eradicate the devastating effects of cancer. From many years of extensive research, we now have some effective ways to control or even cure some types of the disease. Yet, early detection, we are cautioned, is an essential component leading to a cure.

Countless great minds and millions of dollars have been used for decades to develop diagnostic tools for the detection of this often difficult-to-diagnose malady. Most research is focused on the most common forms of cancer. But what about the other debilitating varieties that could greatly benefit from early detection?

In a small cozy medical office in Northern California, an amazing discovery was made utilizing the extraordinary olfactory senses of one dog on a human patient.

While sipping tea in the waiting room before her appointment, a sweet and very friendly dog bounded up to Karole and started to lick her leg. She shooed Fido away, but a determined instinct drew him back to that same spot. The embarrassed receptionist, mumbling excuses, took the frisky puppy into another room.

Some weeks later our tea drinking friend, encouraged by the dog's behavior, had the spot on her leg checked out. The results of the examination confirmed that the very same place where Fido was incessantly sniffing and licking was diagnosed as melanoma, a virulent type of skin cancer.

The very clever dog had, through his very honed sense of smell, detected the presence of cancer, assisting in early detection!

After numerous accounts of similar events, it seems to be a feasible assumption that a dog's sniffer could be a viable diagnostic tool. Studies were then designed to assess the accuracy of such an aid. The findings, surprising many, revealed that the detection of certain cancers by the canines were not only plausible but were confirmed with amazing accuracy.

Determining that the act of sniffing and licking was not quantifiable, scientists hypothesized that there must be an odor contained in the cancer patient's breath that a dog's sensitive nose could distinguish. During the study, patients were instructed to breathe into a test tube which was then given to canines to sniff. Following a set of signals taught to them, the dogs were able to communicate the presence of cancer or lack of it from the patient's breath.

Because of these cancer-sniffing canines, medical science is making headway into the early detection of this feared disease. The grateful recipients of the early detection can actually give a pat and a thank you treat to their heroes, something not easily awarded to the inanimate MRI or CT scanner.

Once the proven validity of the testing was established, it became more regulated. Medical professionals unable to measure the dog's ability to smell cancer, have now devised other measurable protocols involving machines deemed more reliable.

Namaste, When I am in a place of love and oneness, I am one with Mother Earth, Namaste.

Without balance in the *Muladhara Chakra*, our ability to trust, wanes. Rising anxiety that we will not have enough to eat or a place to live steals our peace of mind. Our beautiful blue planet becomes the parent rendered unable to foster our needs. Lack of trust leads us to overuse Her resources, leaving Her barren. The intention of giving back or replenishing becomes lost in our false perception of plenty, fueled by a clandestine sense of lack.

When we exhibit kindness to the earth, She showers us with blessings. Today there is much talk about ecology, saving the earth. We must realize that treating our Mother Earth with reverence and respect is not an option; instead, it is a necessity for *our* survival. We have come from her body and depend on her for continued nourishment.

Namaste With Mother Earth

There are many ways to have reverence and love for the earth; some take time, money and skill, and some are very simple.

I have a fond memory of accompanying my spiritual teacher Sri Swami Satchidanandaji, one of the 20th century's great yoga masters, on a walk toward a grand peak in southern Switzerland. Enchanted by the scenery, a small group of us tarried behind Sri Swamiji's lead. As we walked, the damp grass imprinted our footsteps, proving to the earth that we had been there.

As we walked directly behind Swami Satchidanandaji, I was enjoying the beauty of the day and the feel of the soft, slightly damp grass under my feet. I realized that many creatures made their home in that same earth and became aware that the simple act of walking could cause harm to them.

I felt childlike in my wonder. It took me some time to realize that while my feet imprinted on the earth, Sri Swamiji's did not. As he placed his foot on the grass it flattened, just like mine did. It was the next movement that surprised me. As he lifted his foot before taking the next step, the grass perked back up. As I looked over my shoulder at the lawn I had just treaded upon, it remained flat. Curious to see if it was the same for my companions, I glanced over to see that the grass flattened beneath their feet, as well as when they walked.

Perplexed, the three of us approached Swamiji. "Why is it," we asked, "when you walk on the grass it stands back up when you lift your foot, while under our feet it stays pressed to the earth?"

Slowly pivoting, he glanced at our imprints. "Humm" was the only sound that came from him. Not willing to miss the opportunity for an explanation, we gently prodded. A sweet, reverent expression came to his face, and he put his hand on his heart. "It is not the weight of the body that made those steps in the earth, it is the weight of the heart." And then as if in a distant whisper, "You see the grass as a place for you to walk, to get to where you want to go. I have reverence for the earth and She knows it," he said. "Whenever I walk on the earth, I feel I am walking on my Mother's bosom, and I walk with a light heart, leaving no trace of my being there."

I don't know if I'll ever fully understand what happened that day, but the incident clarified how deeply our consciousness to love and respect the earth can be altered with attitude. Even now, as I walk through a park or on grass I am conscious that the earth is my Mother, and I am treading on her bosom.

It is the Namaste moment of realizing that we and earth are one.

Today, it seems almost everyone is aware of how human activity is harming our planet. Yet, how many are making changes in order to combat the effects? Hopefully, our consciousness is encouraging us to incorporate practical ways to reduce our impact: recycling, driving less, buying "green" products, and so forth.

Dipping deep into your heart, cultivate gratitude and reverence for the earth. As that moment with Sri Swamiji suggests, when our actions are fueled by an inner heart-centered consciousness, the greater world is affected in innumerable positive ways.

*Namaste, When I am in a place of love and oneness,
I am one with Mother Earth, Namaste.*

Feel the Connection

Too often, with the busyness of life, even our good intentions alienate us from the earth. Yet, the reality is that we are intimately joined to her. We are not just living on the earth, we are the earth—our bodies, after all, are made up of the earth!

Focusing attention on the everyday gifts that nature gives us can help cultivate reverence for Her. The simplest act, first thing in the morning, of placing our feet on the floor, reminds us of our deep connection to the earth. With this remembrance, a feeling of gratitude and love engulfs us.

At the Muladhara Chakra, survival is our greatest concern. No matter what level of sophistication we have achieved or how intelligent or wealthy we are, when our survival is threatened, we revert to the emotion housed in the base chakra—fear.

In our sophisticated world, life's lessons often lack the ability to calm our fears and bolster our basic survival skills. How many of us could survive being lost in a forest miles from civilization? Would we know what to eat? Could we find shelter from the cold, heat or rain? Is rubbing two sticks really the way to make a fire?

It has become fashionable for organizations and schools to offer basic wilderness survival training. Brave souls don survival gear and apparatus, hopeful they will conquer nature, or at least learn how to stay alive. After lengthy preparation, they are escorted into the woods, where they are left alone to survive and hopefully thrive. The exercise builds character and reinforces the survival instinct of the Muladhara Chakra.

The qualities of the Muladhara Chakra affirm that we exist on this earth. A keen instinct grants us great discoveries on Gaia, which at first seemed impossible. Replacing fear with confidence and armed with a sharp instinct, we courageously venture through the unknown, accomplishing daring feats with ease.

The essential comfort of that existence is knowing we are interconnected with all living things—plants, animals and humans—all sharing this great adventure on earth. Opening to the perception of oneness, we are united with others in our existence and love flows from us and to us.

The day upheld the legends touting the magnificent red hue of the African sky. We had just flown into the Delta region with hopes of discovering yet another eye-opening adventure of this incredible continent. One of the aspects that endeared me to this land was the way the people honored, lived with, and seemed to sprout out of the earth itself. Their ease and acceptance of the constant ebb and flow of nature's changes caused a slight envy. I wondered how I would contend with having to walk five miles, and then the same number of miles on the return carrying a forty-pound jug of water on my head. Yet, they laugh and sing and dance with complete abandonment. This was my third visit to this incredible land, and each time my respect and admiration for the people expanded.

After a short but very bumpy drive in an open vehicle, we approached an embankment where four dugout canoes rested. Welcoming us were four radiant natives eager to be our guides while poling our canoes. Not yet having the experience of being on the Delta waters, we were keen to float for a while, especially after the free "African massage" in the Jeep.

As we climbed into the boats, we felt embraced by the earth as our boatman began to push the long pole into the muddy delta bottom and we began to effortlessly glide through the reeds. Our only protection was a thin, very thin, unstable shell and our prayers. My intention was to let the road-weary fatigue dissipate; instead, I felt a heightened vigilance enter my consciousness. To our right, a huge twelve-foot crocodile slipped rather gracefully into the water, the very same water that our small canoe was floating upon. With a few reassuring words from our competent guide, the restful experience returned. Not to be kept in that state too long, my husband, always the adventurer, decided he would like to "pole" the boat himself. He had spent a large part of his youth and adulthood sailing, kayaking, rowing, and even trying his hand with a gondola; he was ready to try something different.

Surprised and a bit doubtful, the professional poler's smile told me he was hoping it was a joke. Not to be deterred, my sweet novice poler asked several times, until permission was granted. "This is not a good place to switch, as there is a group of hippos right here that we do not want to disturb." I agreed completely with that statement.

Farther down the delta, "docked" in the reeds, the nod told us it was time. Cautiously the pole was exchanged with the easily removable seat. Slowly, my husband stood up, finding his balance in the small dugout canoe. He pushed on the pole and freed us from the reeds.

With cautious direction and a steep learning curve, the movement became smooth, causing both passengers to relax. It was quite an amazing experience to be floating on this primitive-style vessel in this ancient land, where it is now thought human civilization began. Being part of this in even a small way, I could feel the earth's embrace.

Glancing up, the astounded looks from our fellow travelers at seeing a novice captaining the boat tickled our sense of amusement. We very quietly laughed. After all, we did not want to disturb the hippos or crocs!

I turned to see how our temporarily retired poler was doing. He seemed to be enjoying himself, but I asked anyway.

"He is a really quick learner at poling," was the initial response. Happy to know he was not feeling nervous, I felt he still had something to say. It was the next comment that touched me on a deep level that reverberated through time.

"This is the first time in my life that, as a black man, I am sitting, and a white man is doing all the work. It feels GREAT!" he said, as his beautiful smile overtook his face.

Respect for one another is only possible when we look

beyond the form, be it the color of our skin, the language we speak, the gender or sexual preference. We meet in the place of oneness when we honor the light in all. By honoring her children, the Mother Earth is honored also.

*Namaste, When I am in a place of love and oneness,
I am one with Mother Earth, Namaste.*

Embracing the separateness of being flung from the comfort of our known existence gives birth to fear. A dollop is needed to enable our basic survival. Our health is assured when we use fear as a tool for survival rather than being used by it. Living in the wilds surrounded by animals surviving on you, fear propels you to get out of a dangerous situation quickly. Even if you don't know how to climb a tree your friend, fear, will trigger an ancient instinct and quick as you can think, "I am in big trouble," you have scampered to the top of a big tree.

Our modern society has crystallized fear, banishing it from friend to foe. Overstimulated, fear drains our nervous system and depletes our immune systems. With the incessant honking of cars, dodging traffic, alarm clocks, fire alarms, threats of war, daily news reports, and so on, we seem to be surrounded by constant tinder for deep anxiety.

It is the function of our nervous systems to react to dangerous situations. The peripheral nervous system presents in two parts, the Sympathetic and the Parasympathetic, often coined as the accelerator and the brake, respectively. One function of our Sympathetic nervous system acts quickly by pumping blood to the extremities. All the while, the nervous system floods the

The Namaste Effect

bloodstream with platelets, a white cell that aids in the clotting of our blood, in case we suffer a physical attack. The term 'fight or flight' seems to describe our nervous system's way of supporting our survival, a way to escape danger. In a threatening situation, we can run for our lives, scurry up the closest incline or choose to fight the intruder. It is an ancient response that protects us today, as it did thousands of years before.

In fact, our valiant protector actually differs in reaction whether it springs from a man's or woman's response. The gender differences play out in our survival, each responding in appropriate ways according to the distinct functions they have in society. The standard example of fight-or-flight described above, has been erroneously characterized for both genders.

Engineered to protect and comfort, a woman who "smells" danger will not always be able to fight or flee, but instead she will "freeze and retreat." Designated the caregiver of small children through biology, leaving them helpless while she flees is not part of her makeup. Instead, inspiring by example, she will become motionless, encouraging the children to do the same. Her fright becomes internalized as she strives to be an example of bravery for the brood she is protecting. After the danger passes, the fear must be abated.

A man's anxiety may be released by shouting, working out at the gym, chopping wood, mowing the lawn, or through other physical means. A woman's clearance of stress most successfully comes through comradery. The term "tend and befriend" indicates the process.

Whatever method she chooses to shake off the aftermath of a perilous encounter, it will include sharing feelings about the event with a friend. The aftermath of the incident will be neutralized through empathy and releasing emotion. From a masculine or feminine perspective, both aspects calm the nervous system, both are valid. The letting go must coincide with your inner knowing.

To endure the overload of negativity coming toward us in our modern times, cultivate the Namaste Effect. By recognizing that we all have hopes and dreams and that we are one, we put fear and anxiety back into its safe grotto.

Taking all this into perspective, I share one of my greatest tests of faith of a survival nature involving the Muladhara Chakra.

> "The heart has reasons that reason knows nothing of" —Blaise Pascal

Why would a middle class, educated, and very independent woman decide to take vows from an ancient monastic tradition that has been transported from a country on the other side of the globe? Great question, but it is the heart, not the mind, that formulates the answer.

Putting the trepidation of the first chakra in its place, I took vows to renounce the world with all its sorrows and pleasures. Trusting completely that my basic needs would be taken care of, I donned the robes of a swami (Hindu Monk) and reveled in eternal vows. I was now that bird of the air or fish of the sea.

> "I take care of all the birds in the fields and the fish in the sea. You are my precious children, I will take care of you also."
> —Old Testament

Having nothing to call my own, I was able to 'borrow' all I 'needed.' Happily, I was now free to delve deeply into my spiritual life and service. What I could not envision was how all this would ill prepare me when once again I was thrust into the secular world, a world that might not revere the spiritual treasures I had accrued.

Leaving the sanctuary of my previous monastic life, I found myself for the first year, 'borrowing' from the goodness of friends, sleeping on their sofas, eating their food, using their cars, until the word was no longer 'borrowing' but became 'scrounging.' It was time to take the essence of survival in hand and look for a place to live.

Rent a place to live? Seems like a normal thing to do, normal if I had had money or a job. But without those essential components, who would rent to me? I did have stellar personal references, a belief in myself, and held the conviction that, with love, anything is possible.

Fitting my personal views of life, I chose one of the most liberal parts of California, liberal and very expensive. Armed with faith and a large stockpile of naiveté, my partner and I began "house hunting."

Continually shocked at the cost of housing, we put fear in our back pocket as we searched for the perfect spot. Feeling disillusioned that no one would rent to us (could they not see our bright auric fields?) our hearts started to drain the nectar of hope.

Then one bright day we saw an ad in the paper; the house sounded like heaven. On a drive-by we marveled at the planter boxes spilling over with bright flowers onto a small brown-shingled cottage.

Discounting the caution to be restrained from praising the house, for fear the price would rise, I popped a note in the mailbox detailing my rapture for this "perfect" home. The process of decorating had begun, at least in my mind.

People would chide, "Why would she rent this to you?" "You do not even have proof that you can make the rent." The mind, easily dissuaded, joined the chorus. Mercifully, my heart chimed in, "She will feel your sincerity and honesty. Trust in yourself and the goodness of the world."

The owner of the house loved my note. Armed with love and trust we went to "negotiate." After our illuminating tale, including our monastic commitment and dedication to our spiritual life, the landlady teared up. "I have been looking for special people to be in my home. I know I must be practical to pay my mortgage, but I feel in my heart that you are the ones."

Continuing our bonding, she ushered us to the window overlooking the front yard, which she proudly told us had been the home to a wonderful lama. I was more than a bit shocked that she would keep a monk outside in the elements. Doubt reared its head and caused me to wonder if renting this home from her was really the right decision. After all, I also had very recently been a monk and did not relish the thought of living outside, even in a temperate climate. Gathering courage, at the same time hoping my speaking out would not spoil this wonderful opportunity, I asked, "Why did you not invite him into the house?"

The laughter from my two companions confused me. It seemed like a valid observation to me. After much hilarity it was clarified that it was the animal, llama, not the monk, lama, that had been her houseguest.

As the confusion clarified, the next obstacle loomed. She needed to justify to her life partner why she would rent to a couple who had no viable income or savings and had just left the monastery.

"Are you out of your mind? Renting to people who have no job, no money, but are sweet and loving people? What if they do not pay their rent, we could lose our home?" her partner tried to reason.

"You are going to have to trust me on this one. My heart is saying they are the perfect people for our house; somehow they will attract the right amount to pay expenses. And my heart is now ruling," our future landlady said, standing tall.

It was just the home to shelter us during this time of transition. I am proud to report that the cottage was ours, and the rent was paid on time every month!

After a time, the communion of our body, mind, and emotions with the earth will bring a shift in our inner and outer worlds. It will help each of us find ways to heal Mother Earth. And with the healing of Mother Earth we, her children, are healed.

It is in this Namaste moment that we realize we are one.

> "Come forth into the light of things. Let nature be your teacher."
> —William Wordsworth

Namaste, When I am in a place of love and oneness, I am one with Mother Earth, Namaste.

Meditation on the Muladhara Chakra

● ● ● ● ●

Allow the body and mind to become quiet.

Feel yourself softening into a deep stillness and peace.

Close the eyes.

Take in a few deep breaths and let them out very slowly.

Begin to venture to the base of the spine, to the *Muladhara Chakra*.

There you will find awaiting your awareness a whirling vortex of energy vibrating and radiating a brilliant red. This color vibration generates outward as the *Muladhara Chakra*.

From the base of the spine, feel energy moving downward, rooting directly into the earth. Notice how this energy connects us to the force of Mother Earth, to our basic survival. (a few moments)

From Her body and elements, our bodies are created. The energy entwines and draws us to her as gravity drawing energy from Her to sustain life. She blesses us through the food we eat. Protects us through the clothing we wear and the shelter that safeguards. We thrive on the planet earth.

Observe your breath as it flows in and out with ease.

Feel the energy coursing down from the center of your body and down both legs as they sprout branches from the bottom of the feet, transmitting energy to,

The Namaste Effect

and attracting energy from, Gaia. The ass
survival. (a few moments)

Feel a slight movement, even a tingling, taking place
at the base of the spine.

From this center of survival, the sense of smell
develops, coordinating directly with the organ of
sense, the nose. This direct connection links to our
memory.

Begin to imagine a pleasant smell, perhaps from your
childhood, that kindles up a memory activating all
the cells of the body, igniting pleasant feelings and
sensations. A smile lights the face.

If you are unable to recall the smell exactly, just
imagine the smell and it will kindle the memory. (one
minute)

Leave now the childhood memory and allow the mind
to meander to an adult memory. Was there a time that
you received flowers and the feeling of being loved
was deeply ensconced in your memory by the fragrant
aroma?

Become aware of the entire body as a memory bank,
tingling with that precious feeling. The mind is flooded
with red, the color of love and our life's blood. Take a
moment to allow that experience to infuse your entire
being. (one minute)

Now invoke the scent that allows you to recall a
fearful event. Notice how that feels in your body. Is it
the same soothing feeling as the experience of being
loved and nourished? Observe the unpleasant feeling.
(a few moments)

Nischala Joy Devi

Once again invite the pleasant feeling back to the forefront of your memory.

Allow the unpleasant invocation of fear to fade into the background and return to the sense of hope. (one minute)

You have found the gift of being able to switch to the pleasant when the unpleasant enters into your world.

Gently bring the awareness back to the base of the spine.

Honor the *Muladhara Chakra* for being the connection to the Earth that sustains us.

Make a silent affirmation to nurture the *Muladhara Chakra* and the qualities it holds.

It is honored when we care for our basic needs and for our Mother Earth.

• • • • •

Namaste, When I am in a place of love and oneness, I am one with Mother Earth, Namaste.

Chapter Two

Swadhisthana Chakra

When I am in a place of love and oneness

I am creative and embrace loving relationships

Creativity and Relationships

As Two Become One

One starry night, two divine beings in human form look into each other's eyes. Their love sparks the cosmic essence, igniting the invitation for a new soul to join the Earth's society.

Mother Nature obliges by invoking passion, which leads to the largest and the smallest cell in the human body to enter into a cosmic dance. As one patiently waits, the other swims drunkenly toward the creative energy. Merging, two very different cells, previously unknown to each other, overcome all odds, to become one. A miracle occurs; from two, a third being is created. The union has compelled the divine energy to create a new human being.

WE ARE ONE!

Namaste, When I am in the place of love and oneness, I am creative and embrace loving relationships, Namaste.

The Swadhisthana Chakra

Ascending from the *Muladhara Chakra*, we embrace the *Swadhisthana Chakra*, Dwelling Place of the Self. The first part or the word, *swa*, relates to one's higher self. This is the third level of consciousness. As the first line of the Sacred Gayathri Mantra explains to us, *Bhur* is the earth, *Bhuva* the heavens, and *Swa* is the level of consciousness that is beyond both heaven and earth. Traversing earth and heaven, this chakra has the ability to take us beyond the conventional awareness to remember who we really are.

The *Swadhisthana Chakra,* housed in the spine hovering near the reproductive organs, relates to the water element, the ability to flow. It manifests a range of emotions, creativity, socialization, passion, and group interaction. This chakra is rooted in duality and manifests outward as pairs of opposites. It exhibits a desire to reunite, returning to wholeness, while constantly striving for harmony and balance. These traits grant us the capacity to manifest harmony or disharmony as we form relationships with ourselves and others.

When we focus on the *Muladhara Chakra's* yearning for survival, there is little chance to experience the sweetness of life often associated with the *Swadhisthana*. Enmeshed in constant thoughts of survival, the urgency to fulfill our simplest needs can be all encompassing. When basic survival needs are satisfied, the ability to experience other chakras becomes possible. Moving into the *Swadhisthana Chakra,* we experience a life laced with sweetness and a deep well of passion which, as life unfurls, ignites a colorful kaleidoscope of emotions.

The Swa*dhisthana Chakra* embraces companionship, friendship, and group dynamics. Realizing our interdependence, we acknowledge the virtues of lasting and dedicated relationships that are the key to a fulfilling life.

Repeated scientific studies have proven that emotional support and understanding allow us to overcome many obstacles and aids in healing both body and mind.

In our clinical trial for Reversing Heart Disease, we found that participants who received continuous support from a partner, family, or a close friend did better on the healing regimen and were relieved of their symptoms at an accelerated rate. It is helpful to have someone to encourage us when life gets bumpy, reminding us that life can be sweet even in change.

In Yoga, this concept is known as *Satsanga*, keeping company of those who share the same values you uphold. This universal concept allows us the solace of knowing whatever life brings, we have emotional support. Observe who you reach out to in troubled times; do you seek comfort from someone who reminds you that life is bitter or from one who believes life is sweet?

Namaste, When I am in the place of love and oneness, I am creative and embrace loving relationships, Namaste.

The Color Orange

The *Swadhisthana Chakra* vibrates as the color orange. Being a secondary color, it is comprised of two primary colors: Red, associated with the *Muladhara Chakra* positioned directly below, and Yellow, representing *Manipura Chakra* directly above. This dynamic color radiates warmth and happiness, furnishing an optimistic and uplifting rejuvenation to the spirit.

Relating to the *Swadhisthana Chakra's* propensity toward groups and socialization, the color orange fosters communication, stimulates conversations.

The secondary hue has very distinct characteristics that coincide with the sense of taste reflected in this chakra. It stimulates the appetite, while it encourages companionship. It conjures up the scene of friends gathered around the kitchen table, talking and enjoying each other as well as the food.

The color is often used as a beacon of warning, due to its ability to be seen in dim light or against the water, making it the color of choice for life rafts, life jackets, or buoys. Temporary highway signs warning about construction or detours in the United States are done in this hue, because of its visibility. Even the Golden Gate Bridge is painted *international orange* to make it more visible in the fog.

Both Buddhism and Hinduism adapted an aspect of orange, saffron, for their monastic orders. The brightly colored robe is a sign of renunciation worn by monks and holy ones across Asia. It was always curious to me that orange was chosen for monk's robes, when the *Swadhisthana Chakra* holds the attribute of social interaction. Monks are discouraged from engaging in close relationships, rather are encouraged to remain contemplative without forming attachments to others. Yet, orange is worn, which seems to be a contradiction; perhaps it is worn for visibility, so they can be called into action at any moment.

The Sense of Taste

The *Swadhisthana Chakra* manifests the sense of taste, giving us the ability to enjoy the food that Mother Nature provides, as well as to taste the sweetness or bitterness of life. Combining the element of water with the sense of taste, allows us to delight in our food. Ever tried to eat something very dry, like stale bread? It is not only difficult to swallow, it appears to be void of taste. If we are able to combine the sense of taste with the element of water, we savor the food, thereby receiving the nutrients necessary to thrive. While all five tastes (sour, salty, pungent, sweet, bitter) may be experienced, the primary taste for humans is sweetness. Perhaps that is one of the reasons this chakra is dubbed, sweetness.

Most people enjoy sweet tastes. From the newly born to the long survivors, giving sweet candy, cookies, or cake rewards us with a big smile. Often accused of being an acquired taste, the desire for sweets is inherent from the very first suckle. Human mother's milk contains high quantities of lactose, a sugar. From the very onset, we are given the perpetual message, sweetness and comfort are inseparable. When fed directly from our mother's body, the physical food is only enhanced by the flowing love. As we are embraced and loved, the sweetness of the food sustains not just our bodies but our entire lives.

Saint Francis of Assisi, touted for his deep faith and ability to connect with animals, is also known for his great austerities. Often seen putting ash in his food to obliterate any remnants of good taste, as it also quelled the temptation to eat more than necessary, he was constantly striving to control his senses.

At the end of his life he evaluated, in retrospect, the

peaks and valleys of the landscape of his life. He had built a large following inspired by his great devotion and commitment to protecting God's creation.

One of his devoted students was a woman named Brother Jacoba. We are told she was called brother so he could be close to her without any temptation for physical attraction.

She lovingly cared for him during his final days, his body emaciated, most likely the result of his lifelong austerities. As he lay near death, barely able to speak, he summoned Brother Jacoba. Bringing her ear close to hear his soft words, she was enchanted to hear him ask for cookies. She was regaled for her culinary skills, especially her delicious cookies, of which Francis never indulged.

Hastening to the kitchen to procure the treasured treat, she returned with a plate of her famous cookies. As she broke off a piece and fed him like her precious child, the saint took a bite of the cookie. "Wow! That cookie tastes really good!" was his smiling response.

Even a saint at the end of life, appreciates sweetness! Don't wait—whether with food, people or events, enjoy some sweetness in your life now!

The Water Element—Flow

The element of the *Swadhisthana Chakra* is water, bringing us the ability to flow through life as perpetual movement. The *Muladhara Chakra* comforts us by affording us the steadiness of earth. Feeling grounded, we are now able to invite a flowing energy to steer our lives. As we move into flow, the ability to adapt to different types of situations and people propels us beyond the confines we previously created, to new horizons.

Water has many aspects: cleansing, purifying, relaxing, and nurturing. As a mutable element, it is a challenge to keep it in balance. If too little water, drought can occur; too much, as in flood, can be destructive. Finding the balance in the water element can be tricky because of its natural fluidity.

We can live many weeks without food, but without water our lifespan shrinks to days. Water is essential to our survival, as our physical bodies are composed of up to 60% water. The first nine months of our lives we float in liquid, and from that initiation water continues to comfort us for most of our lives.

Soaking in a hot tub of water allows us to relax. It exudes comfort to children and adults alike. Often, it is even used therapeutically for people suffering from anxiety and other emotional issues. Just the act of soaking in warm water can bring about an emotional change. Others will enjoy a dynamic shower, where it has been said that ideas and thought processes clarify during or after.

As a child, I would delight in putting my nose at the window screen during an afternoon rain shower. The abundance of negative ions filed in through my nose and energized my whole being. Water in all its uses has a way of rejuvenating us.

Thirst is nature's way of keeping the balance of water in our bodies. Many will say that if we wait until we feel really thirsty, we are already out of balance. Those who study such things are now encouraging us to hydrate well before the actual thirst is felt.

In these times, we are becoming acutely aware of the effect of pollution in our water supplies. Causing great concern is the fact that much of our water is literally being poisoned from environmental pollution. We are now spending millions each year to process drinking water, and it is rare to see anyone without a water bottle close at hand. Clean drinking water should be an available commodity for all the citizens of the world, in that the earth is composed mostly of water! We are toying with Mother Nature and she is not happy. We can observe her unhappiness when we encounter flooding in one part of the world while another suffers drought.

I lived in California for many years where the water supply varies greatly. Often plagued with years of drought, the residents learn water conservation early on and practice saving water, whether it is scarce or prevalent. Water is turned on and off during tooth brushing or face washing rather than permitting it to flow down the drain. The daily miracle of having this precious resource, literally at our fingertips, is often taken for granted and waste happens.

Even though I was diligent about water use, I was not prepared for this realization of the blessing of running water. Not everyone takes this daily wonder for granted.

An international worker was touring a small community in Southern Africa. A proud young boy was the docent, explaining the uses and features of the buildings in his ancestral village. With great pride he described each area. "This is the kitchen, an open fire where families cook together. These are the sleeping huts, the shower room."

During the tour, the water source was not obvious. "Where do you get your water from?"

"There is a well in the next village; we walk five miles each way every day for water. The women are all trained from little girls to carry this precious cargo on their heads. They start with just a liter as children and by the teenage years they are able to carry five gallons."

He suddenly stopped talking and reassessed his visitor. "Are you," he hesitated to ask, "from the United States?"

"I am," she answered tentatively.

"I heard a rumor; can you tell me if it is true?" he said.

"Sure, what is it that you have heard?"

"I heard that in your country you have so much water that you actually **pee in it**!"

From the moment I heard this, flushing the toilet has become an act of remembering. I recall daily how precious this miracle we call water is and how fortunate we are to have it so readily available. And never, ever take it for granted!

My husband and I have taken this a step further. Each Christmas instead of giving gifts to friends and family, we pool the money. We then give our holiday money to a charity to dig a well for a small village. Knowing that the people halfway around the globe will have clean drinking water makes our holidays even more blessed.

Tap into this energy by soaking in a natural hot spring or enjoying healing water in your own personal bathtub or shower. Let the water purify your body, mind, and emotions, allowing your spirit to glow.

Namaste, When I am in the place of love and oneness, I am creative and embrace loving relationships, Namaste.

The Emotions Flow Like Water

Water is malleable, changeable, and mutable—a perfect trio to govern our emotional aspect. From the *Muladhara Chakra,* we experience the earth element infusing our physical body with stability, grounded with a sense of survival. We observe the presence of earth energy, in that our physical body appears to change very little and even then at a very slow rate. Often, impatience dominates when a body part or an acute ailment does not heal as quickly as hoped. On the other hand, the emotional body situated in the *Swadhisthana Chakra*, seems to change very quickly. This highlights the different qualities between the two elements of earth and water. Water reflects its fluid qualities, governing the emotional body and its changes.

From the myriad of emotions the human spectrum reflects through the *Swadhisthana Chakra,* the most prominent is passion. Passion is a curious emotion that is able to clearly reflect pain as well as reveal pleasure. Since this is the chakra of duality, pain and pleasure are two sides of the same coin.

We perceive this dualistic switch most dramatically in romantic relationships. Two people meet and fall into deep passion, overflowing with pleasure. Everything pleases them about the other. Their voice, touch, looks, and animal magnetism all lead to the desire for further exploration. At some point something changes; their sweet way of speaking becomes grating. The once sensual touch makes their skin crawl. What happened? The mind, influenced by the water element, reversed the passion, flipping attraction to aversion.

Not only are we influenced by water, we have liquid flowing in our bodies in various forms. These fluids are in constant motion, from the river of life challenging the blood to flow to each and every cell, to the waste products carried out by the urine, perspiration, lymph, and tears. The salty liquids carry the link to our predecessors living in seawater, who ultimately crawled upon dry land bringing within their bodies, the salty sea. If you have a doubt, next time you cry taste one of your tears, or if you prick your finger, taste the blood; the sea is within us.

Tears, being both salty and wet, underscore the emotional spectrum. Upon hearing a devastating diagnosis, my friend's cheek became wet with tears. The physician offering the verdict, choosing not to involve *his* emotions, admonished her for exhibiting hypersecretion of the lachrymal ducts. These ducts aid in the lubrication of the eyes and, in this case, became the clinical description for crying! When truth becomes painful we attempt to deny the emotions, even as the authenticity of tears roll down our face!

With keen observation, we perceive a very fine line between pleasure and pain. It is within that narrow margin that we rely on outside resources to make us feel good, but then in the next moment, through a minor twist in the situation, we feel sad. Similar to a roller coaster, one minute we are at the top of the world feeling happy, the next we are crushed by it, feeling sad. It is this changeable quality that defines passion. Our goal is to keep the element of water flowing in a balanced way. As we find balance, harmony emerges within us. It can then be shared with all we meet, planting seeds for a harmonious world.

The Chakra of Creation

The *Swadhisthana Chakra* encourages the creative energies of the universe to flow through us. It is often said that procreation is the main attribute of this chakra, synonymous with the act of creating another human being. This is undoubtedly one of its finest manifestations, but this dynamic chakra's creativity is only limited by the mind's ability to expand.

In the *Muladhara Chakra,* we are charged with the desire to manifest a place of shelter. Functionality, rather than aesthetics, is the overriding force. Moving into the *Swadhisthana,* the fear of survival retreats, making way for beautification. By building a strong house, creativity may then enter and the decorating begins!

Visiting even the humblest grass-roofed huts or ancient caves previously inhabited, I am awed by the drawings, paintings, or other adornments in these simple dwellings. It is only in the domiciles of humans where such niceties become necessities.

Great artists are notorious for their passion. Would it even be possible to create something memorable and beautiful if passion was missing? Hearing of the exceptional accomplishments of artists in various fields, whether music, painting, sculpture, or writing, the commonality is in the wielding of their great passion. Channeling that passion into artistry, rather than letting it rule, can be a great challenge to creativity.

Much criticism and social scorn is attached to artistic endeavors. In our culture, if anyone expresses the desire or aptitude to dedicate their lives to the arts, they are often seen as immature or even irresponsible, sometimes admonished to "get a real job." Overtaken by practicality, the necessity to anoint our world with beauty and creative expression seems to be, at times, a luxury.

Creative people often vary their expressions between beauty and social discourse, sometimes interweaving both. A master painter, Claude Renoir, chose ordinary people as his subjects, recreating them on canvas as vibrant and more beautiful than in the flesh. Wildly popular in his time, he was inundated with commissions from people who knew the realism they viewed in everyday life would be void from the finished work.

Pablo Picasso, a contemporary master of impressionist art, followed his passion when he painted massive canvases depicting, among other subjects, the political conflict in Spain. As his style evolved, his subjects were often stunned when the finished canvas revealed a disjointed rendition of their symmetrical face and body. Yet, through the creation of a great master, deformed or not, the work was revered.

Marveling at both of these iconic artists today transports us to the essence and passion they infused in their works of art. We do not have to be touted as masters to paint, write, sculpt, prepare a culinary delight, or otherwise create. The creative element in our lives admits us into new realms of expression to enhance and expand our passions.

Namaste, When I am in the place of love and oneness, I am creative and embrace loving relationships, Namaste.

Sex or Procreation?

Human sexuality, a taboo subject for millennia, is now being widely spoken about in casual conversation. In these modern times, sexuality and the pleasure it brings, much of the time, is divorced from what is considered its ultimate outcome—reproduction. By design, the ability to pleasure another is an important aspect in forming relationships and lifelong bonds. Having a clear delineation between pleasure and reproduction allows satisfaction to come through various methods and with an array of partners. It is also the ultimate release, which we are now learning through science sustains health in body and mind. If the desire of the sexual act develops into reproduction, the emotional acceptance that was cultivated is an added bonus.

In humans, as with all animals, certain actions and circumstances need to be present to reproduce. The *Swadhisthana Chakra* holds this important function in its manifold. While humans are able to discern the direct correlation between reproduction and the sexual act, we are told, most animals do not.

With that said, I saw a surprising action performed by a female elephant with her male counterpart, which questioned that edict.

While visiting the Calgary Zoo one fine day, I learned that within the last six months a baby elephant had died. The mother elephant had plunged into grief. Slowly, as the emotional pain subsided, she was ready for another pregnancy. The male elephant, however, apparently had no interest in either sex or fathering.

As I watched, the female seductively danced around her chosen mate, hoping to arouse him. He showed no outward interest. Not easily deterred, she snuggled close to him and, with her nimble trunk, reached under and between his legs and found his fifth leg. Small and flaccid she began to slowly create an up and down motion that caused a sudden expansion. As his interest increased, she positioned herself for the action that would give her the desired effect.

As humans we tend to be a bit more coy. Much effort goes into the courting of another. Elephants are not concerned about how they look or act as far as attraction goes. When a female cat goes into heat the male cat doesn't care what she looks like or how smooth her coat is—the urge wins out. Humans however, go to extremes and much expense to create an image that they feel will attract the attention they crave.

Much of the time, we tend to be charmed by people who are physically attractive. This, of course, varies greatly according to our social training and what our culture deems attractive. In some cultures, it could be physical strength, others wealth, others facial features. The attraction we experience as skin deep, is actually stemming from a much subtler level.

Observing someone dirty and unkempt, our tendency would be one of aversion, probably avoiding an embrace. Whereas if someone clean and attractive caught our eye we would be more likely to look twice. This is not just classical beauty, as we are taught, but our own particular idea of who we consider attractive.

> "Beauty cannot be judged objectively, for what one person finds beautiful or admirable may not appeal to another." —Proverb

This all becomes confusing when we perceive sexual magnetism as solely based on physical attractiveness. If we listen to magazines, TV ads, and the cosmetic industries, we are unattractive unless we look a certain way. If the image of super models or sports figures does not match the reflection we see in the mirror, we feel we are unlikely to get a good catch.

The nature of the physical body is to change. Through the younger years we grow, mature, and develop into attractive adults. As time continues, it brings with it a more radical change of body. Some of the areas that were firm and strong tend to turn soft and saggy. The once firm buttocks move south a few inches as the flat belly rounds. With all this change, are we still attractive? Should the process of ageing, illness, or weight gain rob us of a passionate sex life?

I overheard a man speaking to his recently pregnant wife. "You are glowing. You take my breath away." Sweet, until he added, "You better not get fat and sloppy, or I might not love you anymore." The shocking words returned to my mind a few months later when, after his wife delivered their baby and she was still carrying 'mommy weight,' he found someone new to take his breath away, and divorce was the result.

This or a similar scenario repeats too many times in our society, but when working with women with breast cancer, it turns even uglier. Before breast reconstruction surgery was perfected and popular, many women would refuse treatment for cancer because of the disfigurement it can cause. Their breasts were a large part of defining their sexual attractiveness and beauty. Unfortunately, there were some men who reinforced this myth and rejected their girlfriends and even life partners at the time they needed them the most.

Much time is spent counseling these women that real beauty comes from within and urging them to be attentive to their medical needs rather than superficial beauty. Too many times, with bated breath, I listened to the horror stories of women being rejected by their partners, who took on another after her life altering surgery.

This may be the reason this one story touched my heart.

A devastating diagnosis sent Courtney into a deep depression. Her stellar support team included her husband of twenty-one years. She prepared for the surgery with hope, prayer, and practical advice. With constant reassurance from her husband of his unwavering love, she was fortified with strength. Surgery successful, she readied for discharge. The reality of the surgery deepened while dressing, her blouse revealing an asymmetry. The quick glimpse of herself in the mirror revealed a body that she deemed was no longer sexually attractive. Stifling a sob she turned, shielding the incisional site and asymmetrical chest from herself as much as from her husband's view. She slowly and carefully finished dressing and, leaving the hospital, she tentatively slipped into the passenger side of the car.

Arriving at their home, her gallant husband opened the car door and helped her out. But what happened next changed the course of her healing and ultimately her life.

As they arrived at the front door, as if she was his new bride, her groom picked her up in his arms and carried her over the threshold. Not setting her on her feet, he continued to carry her up to their bedroom and without hesitation made tender, yet passionate love to his "bride" reminding her that she is still attractive and deeply loved. A prince among men!

Namaste, When I am in the place of love and oneness, I am creative and embrace loving relationships, Namaste.

In order to continue the species, the sexual act of reproduction has been designed to be pleasurable, very pleasurable. However, there are still many places in the United States, and abroad, where the act is meant to be pleasurable for only one of the sexes.

Sexual pleasure has, up until recently, been a taboo for enjoyment among women. Trained to be docile, pretending to enjoy or not, women are now coming into their own power. With all that, sex has for centuries been used to control and degrade women for desiring the pleasure easily afforded to men. As women become educated about how their own bodies work and their needs, they in turn are educating their partners.

With the advent of birth control, women are freer to experiment with various partners and methods. In other words, women are finally gaining the privilege to enjoy sex as much as men.

Did you ever wonder if what you felt was love or just sexual attraction? A friend of mine describes how her relationship with her husband formed; rather than saying they fell in love, she says they fell into lust! After five children, she was convinced that the lust did turn into love.

The word *love* tends to be confusing as we use it so commonly. We can love our car, love our computer, love our mother, and love our partner. But it is not the same love that we will explore in the *Anahatha Chakra*, the heart chakra. That love is beyond conditions. "I love you" is a complete statement, not a dangling thought waiting for a reason. Whereas, in the *Swadhisthana Chakra,* the drive for continuing the species is primary, the love conditional. Our concept of love becomes a dualistic magnetism that leads to attraction *or* aversion.

Interestingly enough, much of the shaming and taboos about sex stem from the religious communities. Through the ages women have been dubbed the seductresses that lead a man away from God into sin. There is much historical data that rejects the misconception, but sex and women seem to still emerge as the enemy.

Clever inventors have created devices that allow us to torture the flesh in an attempt to prevent carnal thoughts and actions from manifesting. Enjoyment was considered verboten, yet our bodies are designed to derive pleasure from the act. In spite of it all and the efforts to prevent it, the population continues to grow and passion still reigns.

Monastic communities formed by various religions obliged their members to take vows, among them the promise to remain celibate for life. Celibacy presents itself in various forms.

Natural celibacy is an evolutionary process. You have known and expressed physical passion and may have shared that passion with one or many partners. At a certain time, you may choose to express that passion once reserved for physical pleasure for other creative endeavors or perhaps a relationship with the higher self. The transition is effortless, a natural evolution, that encourages the sexual desire to transform. The intimacy created during the relationship still remains, as witnessed in longtime committed relationships.

The desire for sexual intimacy is very individual, I've seen people later in life continue to have a great sex drive. It has been long assumed that women after menopause have no interest in sex, and that is now being loudly refuted. With the fear of pregnancy abated, the one vital aspect that remains for these liberated women is pleasure.

Many men seem to retain the urge into their later years. We hear tales of seventy-plus year old men fathering children. Of course, the women are much younger! I have seen men literally on their deathbeds in hospitals still flirting with the nurses. And we always say in the hospitals, when they do that, they are getting better!

Religious or socially imposed celibacy can have negative repercussions. From a chakra perspective, imposing celibacy does not necessarily enliven the chakras related to our spiritual union. Rather, it can greatly inhibit the ascension of energy to the Heaven Chakras because of the constant effort it takes to restrain the mind or body. In other words, celibacy is not only physical; the mind and emotions must be in agreement for the energy to continue to flow.

Often, in groups where this vow is enforced, repression manifests as conflict with peers, infighting, jealousy—all accompanying a constant struggle to control the force that propels the world forward.

The *Swadhisthana Chakra,* while espousing the force of procreation, encourages us to live harmoniously with others. This is one of the reasons it has been traditional, whether in a monastic or even educational setting, to house the genders separately. But what about relations among the same sex? Life in community can be very complicated and isolating. Holding to the highest truth of this chakra, harmony above all else, even the great saints who themselves adopted celibacy saw it as "a path against nature."

We hold tight to our beliefs, often formed in childhood. Most children are not encouraged to think for themselves, but entering adulthood our life's experience changes as minds and vistas open. Whether you choose to be sexually active or not must be a personal decision based on your nature and situation; always honor your highest self.

Travel expands the mind and heart to encompass a greater understanding of the way different cultures experience life and especially intimacy.

What is taboo to one culture is commonplace to another. The social norms cannot be judged from our societal edicts when on the other side of the world. Are we able to embrace others as ourselves if they are unable to conform to our expanded or limited thinking? If we can accept another's ways and lifestyles, our inner and outer worlds will grant us the harmony we crave.

Let's Rewrite This

A young scribe was summoned to an ancient monastery in a distant land. His task was to copy by hand a holy book engraved on palm leaves that had been kept for posterity. It was a long and arduous assignment, and he was determined to make it as accurate as possible.

When the old abbot presented him with the previously copied scriptures, he rejected them. "I want to see the originals; often mistakes are made, and without the original they can be repeated into perpetuity."

The abbot resisted, knowing how difficult it would be to find the originals not seen for possibly hundreds of years. The scribe, unwavering in his resolve, insisted on the original, and as the project desperately needed to be done, the abbot relented. Slowly and with great struggle, the head monk hobbled down the stone steps to the archives below the great monastery in search of the original works.

The scribe patiently waited for a few hours until his patience turned into irritation. What could be taking the old monk so long? It is getting dark and I will not be able to work at all today. The hours continued to pass as the irritation now morphed into concern.

Trying to remember the pathway to the archives, the young man cautiously climbed down the same stone steps that the abbot trod, many hours before. Reaching the dimly lit archives, he was able to make out a small figure laying on the ground, murmuring.

On closer inspection the figure on the floor was the old abbot. He was banging his head against the stone floor and mumbling incoherently.

"What is it?" said the scribe. "Are you hurt? Can I help?"

Continuing to exclaim more vehemently, "I cannot believe it! All these years of needless suffering and misunderstanding!"

"What is it? Can it be so awful?"

"You were right to find the original; the copies are all wrong," said the abbot as he proclaimed, "The Scripture says to **Celebrate**, not to be **Celibate**!!!"

Namaste, When I am in the place of love and oneness, I am creative and embrace loving relationships, Namaste.

It seems as we revolve in our very busy circles of daily living, we have little time to connect with each other. Even among many of my more conscious friends, finding time to socialize is at the bottom of the priority list. Work time has taken over our social time.

Keeping company with those who share your values and encourage you to live your highest potential is the

Yogic concept called *Satsanga*. It is such an important precept that some of the masters say that by *Satsanga* alone you can realize you own true self. How could that work?

Readying to go to a very special occasion, you imagine yourself looking attractive and stylish in a certain outfit that you bought last year. Hopes are dashed as no amount of tugging on the zipper will convince it to close. The only hope is to go on a diet 'til the zipper slides like silk. Having made the resolve to count calories, you receive an invitation for a pizza party. What to do? One part wants to go, to be with friends and have a fun time; the other fears eating too much, causing the dreaded zipper to remain in two parts.

Calling your dear friend, the hostess of the party, you explain the situation—wanting to go, yet not wanting to go. "I totally support your effort to lose those pounds. I will make sure there are plenty of salads and will encourage you to eat the foods that are in alignment with your goals. We are here for you 100%."

That is the power of *Satsanga*. Supporting us with positive advice and advocating for our highest goals, ranging from the mundane to lofty spiritual attainments. In this world of contradiction and competition, finding those who attest to our highest is comforting and empowering. The somewhat contradicting ideas of individuality vs. dependence is often offset by a feeling that we need each other to thrive. This is the ability to stand together, not entwined.

> "One that walks with the wise will be wise, but one that walks with the unwise will harm themselves." —Old Testament

When we look into a forest, each tree appears to stand independently, relying on its roots to pull precious nutrients through the trunk to the branches above. If we had the ability to see just below the soil level, a stunning fact would emerge. While the trees appear to be separate and individual, they, in fact, are joined and interconnected just under the earth's surface. This intricate system allows each root to draw nutrients from the earth both for itself and to share, so all are fed and nourished through a communal effort and cooperation.

We have all heard the biblical saying, *Love thy Neighbor as Thy Self.* Intrinsic in that phrase is the unspoken aspect that we must learn to love ourselves, before we can truly understand how to love our neighbors.

Usually the phrases quoted in the Bible or other Scriptures are not easy to do, otherwise, why would they be included? These words of wisdom are there to help us purify our minds and bodies, so the spirit can shine through. But, even with people who have made it their life's work to serve others, blind spots can be found.

A simple experiment was enacted one Sunday morning. In a small town several ministers, each having their own parish, received calls at 8 a.m., alerting them that the minister scheduled to give the Sunday morning sermon at their church fell ill. Could they be there by nine o'clock and fill in for their colleagues? Willing and ready to serve, the majority of ministers leapt into action. With needing to shower, breakfast, and get to the church, there was no time for sermon preparation.

The ministers were asked to offer a sermon on the Good Samaritan. Recalling, the story took place in the town of Samaria where the people were thought to be selfish and narcissistic. It is about a traveler who is stripped of clothing, beaten, and left half dead alongside the road. A few pass the injured man, but they avoid him. Finally, one Samaritan happens upon the traveler and helps the injured man. The action was so important that the entire story was added to the Bible and he became known as the Good Samaritan. In thinking this over, it may seem that such acts of kindness would be common. Yet are they?

With great time pressure, the ministers were preoccupied trying to formulate a sermon en route. Part of the experiment was to intentionally place obstacles in their path as they hurried to their respective churches.

A fretting woman approached one minister, saying she was lost and needed help. He quickly told her he did not have time to assist, as he was already behind schedule.

The next found a man looking for a lost child; he received the same rejection from yet another minister on his way to give the sermon.

The most extreme was a man pretending to be passed out on the sidewalk, so the minister literally had to walk around him. And he did!

All this to give a sermon on the Good Samaritan! These ministers normally were kind and service-oriented people. What then happened? Time pressure and stress can alter our minds and confuse our hearts, as they confused the hearts of the ministers. When the task at hand becomes more important than the people right in front of us, we need to pause and make a course correction.

We must make people and our connection with them top priority in our lives. Then, we have created a heaven on earth.

"What wisdom can you find greater than Kindness?" —Jean-Jacques Rousseau

Namaste, When I am in the place of love and oneness, I am creative and embrace loving relationships, Namaste.

Meditation on the Swadhisthana Chakra

• • • • •

Allow the body and mind to become quiet.

Feel yourself softening into a deep stillness and peace.

Close the eyes.

Take in a few deep breaths and let them out very slowly.

Observe the energy coursing from the top of your head, moving downward through the body, and settling in the *Swadhisthana Chakra* at the center of the lower belly.

There, you will find awaiting your awareness a whirling vortex of energy vibrating and radiating a brilliant orange hue.

This color vibration generates outward as the *Swadhisthana Chakra*.

Meaning sweetness or dwelling place of the Self, it connects us to the energy force of creativity and relationships.

Feel a slight tingling at this vibrant chakra.

From this dynamic force, we are able to create a beautiful work of art, a delicious meal, or even another human being. When balanced, the energy allows us to commune with other souls in a way that brings healing and love.

Recall a delicious taste, perhaps from your childhood,

that kindles up a feeling activating all the cells of the body, igniting pleasant feelings and sensations. Feel a smile light the face.

If you are unable to recall the taste exactly, just think of the taste and it will kindle a feeling. (one minute)

Leave now the childhood memory and allow the mind to meander to an adult experience. Was there a time that you received a sweet treat and the feeling of being loved was deeply endorsed by the mouthwatering taste? Become aware of the entire body as it tingles with that precious feeling. (a few moments)

Allow the mind to flood with a vibrant orange, the color of creativity and a sense of belonging. Take a moment to allow that experience to infuse your entire being. (one minute)

Now, invoke the sense of taste that allows you to recall an unpleasant event. Notice how that feels in your body. Is it the same soothing feeling as when you experience a pleasant taste? (one minute)

Observing the unpleasant feeling, gently re-invite the pleasant feeling to the forefront of your memory. As you do, allow the unpleasant sensation to transform into a pleasant feeling. Allow the ability to create your own reality to return. (one minute)

Take in a few deep breaths.

You have given yourself the gift of being able to switch to the pleasant when the unpleasant enters into your world. ● ● ● ● ●

Namaste, When I am in the place of love and oneness, I am creative and embrace loving relationships, Namaste.

Chapter Three

Manipura Chakra

When I am in a place of love and oneness

I am empowered and empower others

The Power and the Intellect

Are We One?

One night, after an inspiring Yoga class, Jim was heading home. His usual mode of transportation was the subway. The underground train's vibration did not support the way he felt after leaving a relaxing class. The closing words from his teacher, "We are *all* Divine" accompanied by the *Namaste* greeting to each other, had expanded Jim's heart. He descended the long stairs to the underground platform. Finding the station abandoned at this advanced hour, he continued to repeat the phrase as he savored the memory of the oneness he felt.

The phrase was abruptly paused by flashing blades held by four rather disturbed-looking men. As they surrounded him, the fate that was being projected made his heart pound with fear. "Take my wallet, my money, anything; please leave me unharmed." The plea only brought them closer. The vacant platform consumed any remaining hopes for survival.

As if from a faraway tunnel in his consciousness, he began to hear, "We are *all* Divine." Diverting his attention to the affirmation rather than the scene surrounding him, his heart began to calm.

Fueled by intention, the declaration took on greater power. "We are *all* Divine." It was now pounding in his ears and head, overshadowing the outer words being shouted at him. "We are *all* Divine."

Unknowingly, he began to speak the words aloud. "We are *all* Divine."

"What did you say?" growled one of the assailants.

"We are *all* Divine," Jim repeated, this time with more gusto. "Brothers, you and I, we are *all* Divine. If you hurt me, you are hurting yourself." He was now looking at the four, not as his attackers but as his *own* Self. "We are *all* Divine," his conviction accelerating.

Time began to slow down, and he thought his eyes were deceiving him. With clear sight, he watched the four men sheath their knives and run toward the oncoming train.

Still repeating, "We are *all* Divine," Jim became conscious of being alone and safe on the subway platform. We ARE *all* Divine had become his conviction and savior.

The affirmation that abated the fear was now fading. He had been saved not by his might or quick wit but by the openness of his reverent heart, which had allowed him to see even his would-be attackers as his own self. Real life grants miracles every day.

When even hearing of dramatic situations like this one, we become overwhelmed with gratitude for the preciousness of life. And we realize how, in a heartbeat, it can all be gone.

Namaste, When I am in the place of love and oneness, I am empowered and empower others, Namaste.

The Manipura Chakra

The *Manipura Chakra*, meaning lustrous gem, is reminiscent of the sun at the center of the celestial system we live in. It manifests as the fire element, a resplendent source of power, which affords us the ability to think, reason, experience, learn, and enjoy great vitality.

To understand the *Manipura Chakra,* we look to its location in both the physical and subtle bodies. The subtle energy system, while quite complex, is the blueprint that allows for the physical body to manifest its many functions.

On a physical level, the *Manipura Chakra* radiates outward at the solar plexus just below the diaphragm. The diaphragm is a large hemi-domed muscle that divides the thoracic or chest cavity from the abdominal cavity. On the subtler level, it serves to segregate the Heaven Chakras from the Earth Chakras.

The *Manipura Chakra* forms the apex of the "Earth" chakras in that, from there, the energy flows downward through the *Swadhisthana* and *Muladhara Chakras*. This subtle downward flowing energy is known as *apana-vayu*, returning to the main energy source, the earth.

The strategic placement of the *Manipura Chakra* allows this energy vortex to manifest the subtlest of the earth elements—fire. While the energy source of this chakra still has a downward manifestation, it is from here that we can begin to cajole the energy to move upward.

Directly above the *Manipura* is the *Anahatha Chakra;* it is from here that the first of the upward energies, called *prana-vayu*, originate. The *prana* and *apana* respectively, being opposing energies, manifest different aspects and destinations. The *apana-vayu* offers the grounded-ness of the earth and all of her gifts, while the *prana-vayu* reaches for the grandeur of heavenly influences and all the sublime qualities it holds. Two opposing energies, by design, lead us to the source.

The ability to think and reason are two gifts that humans possess, distinguishing us from other species. Through this process, we gain the ability to problem solve and assess, whether situations sprout from the outside or from within our bodies or minds.

The intellect and the fire element go together like hand and glove. Observing someone problem solving is like looking into their mind and seeing their thought process. All the inventions, even the discovery of fire itself, sprang from this great power. Societies who wield influence, not only within their own country but throughout the entire world, most often vibrate in this chakra.

At this moment in time, a strong intellect is the reigning monarch. Our whole fascination with electronics, computers, robots, space travel, etcetera fuel and are fueled by this great firestorm housed in the *Manipura Chakra*. When the knowledge gained is used benevolently, it is heralded as a great discovery. However, if this power is channeled into destruction, as in the manufacture of more powerful bombs and weapons, we must take a step back, evaluating its role.

I worked with a caring and compassionate physician, who confessed he chose medicine for an unusual reason. As a younger man at university, he had majored in physics. Being intellectually keen, he quickly was recognized for his skill level. He was offered a lucrative position to work on a secret venture, so secret even those immersed in the project did not know the implications. When the A-bomb was detonated in Japan to end World War II, he understood that he had played a major part in the destruction of lives and land.

Unable to rationalize his participation in such a heinous act, he plunged into righteous indignation. Wrestling the anger for control, he chose to return to university and specialize in medicine; this way, his education could be used to save lives instead of annihilating them.

The power of the *Manipura Chakra* is malleable and can lend itself to be equally effective for the greater good or greater harm. As we explored the *Swadhisthana Chakra,* we observed that by expressing emotions encased in the water element we tended to be more pliable, easily moved by situations and events, thereby reflecting the attribute of flowing water.

Moving into the element of fire, the malleability factor of the previous chakras is now replaced with strength, power, and reason. Much of our thinking and reasoning skills are developed by our early twenties, when many people have completed a level of well-rounded education.

"I think therefore I am," professed René Descartes, a French philosopher, mathematician, and scientist, dubbed the father of modern Western philosophy. This concept took off, propelling the western world into a level of arrogance that only rivaled the misinterpretation of the biblical phrase, "Let man (or woman) have dominion over the fish in the sea and the birds in the sky and over all the creatures that move along the ground."

Experiencing that biblical quote from a balanced *Manipura Chakra* would predicate care and protection for those we have dominion over, rather than rationalizing that they are there for our personal use or benefit.

Also, a balanced view would caution M. Descartes

to rethink his understanding from the Yogic perspective, where "I think, therefore I am," morphs into "I am, therefore I think."

When there is a balance and radiance of the *Manipura Chakra*, the fire of the internal sun bolsters our self-esteem, liberating benevolent qualities, formulating our place in the world.

A tree grows with the support of sun and water. Absorbing the rays of the sun, it accumulates and stores the sun's power for a future time. When the tree is chopped and split, it is ready to release that stored fuel. In the burning process, the rays from the sun housed unseen in the wood logs release fuel to warm us in winter, cook our food, and supply us with other abundant uses we have for fire power. Similar to a tree, this chakra radiates warmth as well as igniting our intelligence.

The color emanating from this chakra mimics the colors of the sun. When the *Manipura* is strong and balanced, it creates a golden aura that surrounds us. Yellow is considered a color of vitality and allows us to experience cheerfulness and the sense of being uplifted. It is the chosen color in many food establishments where an atmosphere of congeniality is encouraged. Wearing the color often rewards us with a smile that brightens up any gloom.

Our main purveyor of this golden cheer is the sun itself. Imagine emerging after days in the house due to cloudy or inclement weather. You need only to step out of the front door to experience the change in mood. Raising your face up to the warmth and light of the sun immediately soothes the body and rejuvenates the mind as we are reunited with our sunny nature.

Yellow has become a very popular color for kitchens,

something about preparing food while basking in the color of the sun. As the *Manipura Chakra* also governs the organs of digestion, the presence of the solar hue adds to the whole experience. Part of the spectrum of the color yellow, is gold. The color is synonymous with the precious metal that echoes the qualities of wealth and prosperity. With a desire to espouse those qualities, people will often spend vast amounts of money adorning themselves with this shining alloy.

Even when our financial resources are unable to eke out an elaborate home or car, the budget will often allow for a neck chain, bracelet, or bobble made of gold. It uplifts us, elevating our self-esteem, while impressing others. Embarking on the wonders of this chakra, it is impressive the vast spectrum of qualities it radiates.

Namaste, When I am in the place of love and oneness,
I am empowered and empower others, Namaste.

Our personalities are a combination of what we were born with and what we acquire. Combining the aspects of personality with personal power, some traits are inherent while others are learned, and many are reinforced through our behavior or the influence of family and friends. "Tell me who your friends are, and I know who you are," says a popular adage.

When ensconced in our own power, we become steadfast in knowing who we are and are ready to meet anything the world slings at us. With an eye toward fairness, the meeting of these aspects is met with confidence, promoting the ability to solve issues with objectivity toward others and ourselves. The whole field of mediation is based on this premise. There are two sides to every disagreement and it takes three people to resolve it.

From that place of power, we understand that people have different views and expectations. When faced with an unpleasant encounter, we are able to remain clear that we are not the target but the unwilling recipient of a disagreeable energy present in *their* lives. We radiate an unshakable confidence, and others react to that stability.

The flip side to the quality of power is the feeling of being powerless. Whether the impression of feeling inadequate is fostered in childhood or formulated during our teenage years, it sets our image of how we experience and act in the world. When we feel a lack of personal power, our reactions stem from a deep place of insecurity. We perceive that the world as a whole is against us, and we find ourselves constantly on the defense. We develop coping mechanisms that attract relationships based on that lack. Our choice of friends may include those who are less intelligent, so we may appear smarter. Or conversely, befriending pals much cleverer than we, thereby reinforces our lack of self-esteem. Either choice keeps us bound to that original impression of being less-than.

The Abuse and Use of Power

One of the concerns facing many children and young adults today is being bullied. This unkind way of relating was always in our midst, but with the development of the internet and social media it has risen to crisis proportion.

Why would someone want to be a bully, causing undue emotional or physical pain to others? To the onlooker, this seems like a curious, if not cruel, choice. On closer exploration, although bullies purport to be powerful and self-confident, they are actually lacking in self-esteem. Why else would they choose to denigrate the vulnerable? Someone who stands in their power would choose to protect, not harm. In an effort to compensate for our lack of power, we often idealize another, use an additive substance or any means to artificially bring us the power we crave.

Aikido is a synthesis of martial arts, philosophy, and religious beliefs. It was created to enable the practitioners to defend themselves, while also protecting their attacker from injury. Aikido is often translated as "the way of unifying" or "the way of harmonious spirit."

It is one of the great spiritual practices akin to Yoga in that, when mastered, it allows the purveyor to accept negative energy from another, transform it into positive energy and then return it back to the donor. It is unusual in the sense that when most of us encounter negative energy, we either absorb it into us or return it amplified to the sender.

On a peaceful weekend morning, an accomplished Aikido Master was seated in the back of a crowded train for her nature outing. Sitting quietly, she noticed a very large and quite inebriated Sumo wrestler coming aboard.

Forcing his way into a seat between two people, he began with verbal abuse. Fear crept through the overstuffed train and, with little room to spare, people started to seek refuge. Because of his girth, when he sat he overflowed onto the next seat. Plopping down in a front seat, he pushed an elderly couple into the side wall. The absent apology was replaced by a loud grunt as he settled in. Some of the passengers began to stare and whisper, which unnerved the man even more, causing him to spout coarse language and gestures. A fearful hush spread through the moving vehicle.

Observing from afar, the situation called for action. Deliberately, the Master rose from her seat in the rear and slowly made her way to the front of the train. Eyeing an empty seat, she installed herself before gesturing to the wrestler to join her. He did not seem eager to move his seat but the Master, with a smile and a pat of the seat, cajoled the man to join her.

As she continued to entice him with kind gestures, the disturbed man finally rose and reluctantly joined the Master in the front row. Inelegantly taking the better part of the two seats, he thrust her against the wall. As her body settled, he continued to rant and spew foul language. With his drunken abuse escalating, the oversized man observed his new seat mate. "Get away from me, you ugly woman, I need the room, I will crush you if you do not."

Unaffected, the brave soul stayed. Within a short time, she began a conversation, "Are you having a difficult time?"

"What is it your business? Leave me alone."

"I know that you are acting this way because you must be hurting."

"I said, leave me alone," and he proceeded to knock the calm woman to the floor. Unperturbed she climbed back into the seat.

Not to be easily swayed she spoke slowly and compassionately, "Sometimes when I am upset about something or someone, I have to be very careful not to project my negative feelings on others. Do you agree?"

"Humph."

"I feel something has you very upset. Would you like to talk about it?" the Master said, tentatively touching the man's arm.

When the wrestler did not pull away or react, the next step was taken.

"Do you want to tell me what you are upset about?"

With a wide-open heart, she leaned closer to the disturbed man. This time, she was not rejected. So she inched closer.

With a great pause and audible sigh, he said, "My mother is very sick, and I am afraid she will die."

A tear slipped from his eye as he related his mother's illness and his feeling of helplessness. "I love her so much. What will happen to me if she dies? I will be all alone."

The Master, cautiously raising her arm to lightly embrace and comfort, said "I know how that feels; I also love my mother deeply and when she is ill, my fears are like yours."

To the amazement of the onlookers, the wrestler slowly bent his head until it came to rest on the Master's shoulder. A cascade of tears from his cheek streaked her blouse.

Embracing the wrestler, the Master held him while he sobbed.

With soft words of comfort and assurance, this small open-hearted woman had recognized that under the anger was a soul in emotional distress. An observer, louder than he meant to, exclaimed, "That is Aikido!"

And that is the Namaste Effect!

A phrase that I formulated years ago, it still serves me each and every day.

"Happy people do not make other people unhappy."

When the feeling of being powerless engulfs us, we may look for something that has the power we crave. Many reach for alcohol, drugs, or other means which encourage a temporary sense of being in control. But what are the consequences of using a substance to bring a false sense of power?

Present in the *Manipura Chakra* is the tendency toward abuse and self-abuse, almost like being your own bully. Without realizing the reason for our addiction, we embrace unhealthy and often life-threatening situations.

The drug and alcohol addiction rates have skyrocketed. We investigate—is it a genetic predisposition? Taught behavior? Whatever the reason, its presence in today's society is having a devastating effect on the individual, the family, and the world at large. While uncovering the cause of the addiction, be it heredity, social pressure, etcetera, the *Manipura Chakra* suggests that feeling powerless is key to unlocking the mystery.

One of the participants in our Reversing Heart Disease Study related this in a clear way. Asked to give up the smoking habit prior to entering the study, he tested our compassion.

"To you," he said, "smoking is an unhealthy and dirty habit. Giving up cigarettes would make sense, knowing that I have heart disease. But what you do not understand is, in this pack of cigarettes I have twenty friends. They are there for me, no matter what happens. If I am feeling blue, they are there. If I am lonely, they bring solace. They never let me down and when they are here with me, I feel less lonely."

The twenty cigarettes that he called "friends" *are* always there for him. People have let him down but the pack doesn't, on an emotional level. However, on a physical level, his "friends" are slowly destroying his body.

It is the same scenario with alcohol. Feeling down and needing a friend, we may visit our "therapist," the local bartender. S/he listens attentively to our feelings and woes. We sit and talk, have a few drinks, then with each new someone who lends an ear, we take a few more drinks. The next day dawns with the same problems, so the scenario of the previous day is repeated without being resolved.

The next time we reach for a drink, it may not be for the social solace but to drown our sorrows drinking alone, at home. The harmful ritual slowly erodes our family, friends, body, and mind and devastates our self-esteem. The whole purpose of drinking to quell our sorrows has failed. The alcohol habit has multiplied the sorrows for us and for those who love us.

Drug addiction seems to target our most vulnerable. Unaware of the dire consequences, the youth, in their illusion of immortality, experiment with an assortment of street drugs. The desire to move into a different reality, any other than the one they are in, pulls them into the illicit world of delusion.

It may begin as a fun time, trying something new, perhaps peer pressure to "not be a chicken." The one-time trial was so satisfying that another is imminent. When one of the lighter drugs seems inadequate, a more powerful one steps up. And so an addiction has begun. Resolving such a habit takes time, vigilance, and much support from family and professionals.

When addiction is rooted in lack of power, it is necessary to infuse the knowledge of being powerful into our youth and population. There needs to be an overhaul of our teaching and parenting methods, to allow each individual to know they are part of the one divine consciousness that is present in everyone. We learn the real power is within; it is the one constant we can count on. When that authentic power is our compass, addiction no longer can weave its web.

Namaste, When I am in the place of love and oneness, I am empowered and empower others, Namaste.

Keeping Anger in a Cave

The main negative emotion associated with the *Manipura Chakra* is anger. This powerful emotion is directly associated with fire. Fire has the capacity to warm us in winter, to cook our food, and to serve us in numerous ways. Yet, when uncontrolled, it destroys everything in its path.

Anger, being born of fire, has the power to extinguish both the one who dispenses it *and* the recipient. Also, it seems to be the gift that keeps giving. Once we have unleashed anger on someone, it is rarely forgotten, even years later. This explosive emotion is fueled by a sense of insecurity or lack of control and power. When our desires are thwarted, we lash out at anyone we might suspect is responsible. Often anger, the offspring of misunderstanding and suspicion, is taken as a personal affront when that was not necessarily the intention. These perceptions are usually accompanied by a less than calm mind.

Anger has a wide spectrum of expressions, from righteous indignation to a full-blown tantrum. Whatever the form, the effects can be detrimental to both the source and the recipient. Regardless, each are affected and often with scalding effects.

While the psychological and social factors present a challenge, it is often the physiological symptoms that make us take notice.

Science tells us that it takes at least three hours for the body to return to a balanced natural state after an angry episode. During anger, we illicit a sympathetic nervous system reaction. This causes platelets, sticky white cells involved in the clotting of blood, to be released. If they are not called into use, they often join in with other fatty cells to cause a blockage—commonly called *plaque*—in the coronary arteries. Various "stress" hormones rush in, affecting the blood pressure, and the delicate balance within the heart is upset. Thus, it seems reasonable for the body to require three full hours to restore balance.

Research confirms that many heart attacks happen within three hours of an angry episode. Once stabilized, patients brought into emergency with a heart attack were asked when their last angry episode occurred. Overwhelmingly the answer was within the last three hours! Can anyone afford the luxury of anger?

> "A moment's hesitation with anger can save one hundred days of sorrow." —Lao-tzu

Often, we hear of feuds between families or even within the same family that span generations. Trying to understand why Uncle Sal does not speak to Aunt Sally often stumps the younger, uninvolved generations.

Years back, one might have said something unkind or "stole" a sweetheart, and fifty years later the dispute continues, the anger remains palpable. By holding on to their hurt and anger, resolution is a distant hope, betrayal looms large.

Letting go of anger can be quite the challenge, and often we are not adept at it. Drastic measures are often taken to quell the mind and let anger dissipate; often, it is just pushed underneath the surface.

There was a great spiritual teacher who had difficulty controlling her anger. Realizing the harm it was causing to herself and others, she decided to retreat into a cave, taking a vow of silence. Hidden away for many years, the day arrived for her to emerge from the cave. The word spread far and wide, inviting throngs to greet her reentry into the world.

Along with the faithful came some reporters. A statement had been released touting the great accomplishment of the *sadhu* (spiritual seeker) to have completely tamed her anger. All waited impatiently to hear her wisdom. Humbly emerging from the cave, she was immediately confronted by the group.

"Tell us, *sadhu*, are you completely free from anger?"

"Completely gone," said the cave dweller.

"In all the years you were in the cave, not once did anything disturb your peace?" the reporter chided.

"No, nothing," the teacher said, starting to feel a bit shaken.

"Excuse me, but it is difficult for me to believe that in all the time nothing disturbed you, not even an insect or snake disturbed your meditation." The interrogation continued.

"I told you, my peace was undisturbed."

"But, there must have been at least one instance that anger would have reared its head."

"YOU FOOL, STOP QUESTIONING ME, I TOLD YOU I DID NOT EVEN ONCE GET ANGRY. NOW YOU ------GO AWAY AND LEAVE ME ALONE!!!!!!!"

It is quite easy to be peaceful when there is nothing to prod and poke at you. This becomes a very different story when many are ready to contest and interrogate. Is it better to stay in the world and learn to let the small conflicts go? Is it better to save that anger for the times it is really necessary to show your power, if such a time does even exist?

Swami Satchidanandaji would tell us to keep anger in our pockets, and in the rare occasion it is needed take it out, roar like a lion, and then return it to its rightful place, back in your pocket.

The positive emotion of the *Manipura Chakra* to cultivate is happiness. It is a magical attribute that changes all it touches with the power to elevate and enhance. When plagued with anger, look to the lightness of your being, move into happiness, and watch the anger evaporate!

Namaste, When I am in the place of love and oneness,
I am empowered and empower others, Namaste.

Money as Power

Visiting Florence, one of the most beautiful renaissance cities in Europe, I was entranced with its culture and artistic masterpieces. Florence seems to have it all—magnificent cathedrals, indescribable sculptures, and paintings that have the power to put us in rapture.

Strolling in the early evening along the Pont d'Or (Gold Bridge) where all the jewelry stores tout their sparkling wares, a bold sign caught my roving eye.

THE GOLDEN RULE: Those that have the Gold, Rule!

Not the golden rule I was taught in childhood, but maybe the right observation from days of yore to present times. The power that is yielded in the *Manipura Chakra* can be closely attached to who we appear to be in the world and how much that is worth, monetarily.

Politicians, amassing great wealth to fuel campaigns, are often elected not for their merits but based on how many donors they can woo. Where is *their* power, in the money or in their commitment to raise the living conditions of the people they are serving?

Is it okay to have money while others suffer from lack? If money is power, can we who are privileged do something to elevate those in need? The adage, money cannot buy health or happiness, is quite true in its simplicity. Chronic diseases, for the most part, seem to lack discrimination between rich and poor. While it is true of the nature of the disease itself, when it comes to treatment, the rich move to the forefront of care.

The rising cost of medical care has, unfortunately,

hindered the average person from making necessary preventative visits to a health care provider. With regularity, these consultations can prevent some maladies from taking root. Weeded out early, the full-blown disease is averted.

When the choice is between medical care and food for dinner, the pressing need of hunger wins. Those living with enough, and more than enough, are often not aware of those living with a lack of funds. Even if we know of a dire situation, what can we do to help?

The financial circumstances of our childhood impact the way we live our adult life. Even with limited money, many of us experienced our parents' generosity during our formative years. Their examples came with hope that our generosity would exceed theirs.

My father a very unconventional man, preferred to carry his money in his pocket rather than a wallet or even keep it in a bank! Known to many as a generous person, those close to him never wanted for the basics, but luxuries were an uncommon visitor to our home.

As a child, I remember accompanying my mother to the supermarket. She carefully would mark the price of each item before the basket received it. Making sure there was enough money to pay, we would line up for the checkout. Even with her great number skills, more than once she would see the total and with a quiet voice ask the cashier to please take out the butter or other "luxury" item.

Being part of his nature, generosity did not escape my dear father. I recall a business acquaintance approaching my father recanting a dire need for money for his sick child. Without a moment's hesitation, his hand reached into his pocket and emerged with a wad of cash, offering the petitioner to take whatever was needed to assist his child. Without asking for the money to be returned, my father walked away confident that the offering was in alignment with his belief. Both aspects of childhood have grown deep roots in my *Manipura Chakra*. These examples of humility and generosity are two companions that will travel the journey of life with me. How we use our power affects our use of money and its distribution. Money is power. Use it wisely.

On one of the busiest highways in the New York/New Jersey metro area, a toll taker was shown the power of generosity. Edging toward evening, the cars reluctantly slowed to pay the toll on a highway that has charged its users since its inception. Slowing the speed to a complete stop added valuable minutes to commute time. Drivers searching for money or waiting for change all clipped time from theirs and other's family and relaxation.

One average gesture of goodwill changed the day for 250 people, their families and those of us hearing the tale. Pulling up to the toll both, a kind person, instead of taking the change owed to her from the toll, "donated" the coins to pay for the car behind her. Having already retrieved the cash to pay the toll, the next driver, touched by the generosity of the previous toll payer, paid for the driver behind *him*.

The spark of generosity having caught on, the next driver followed in kindness. This phenomenon had occurred many times before, but what made this occasion so special was it lasted, to the toll taker's amazement, for two and a half hours! Non-stop generosity on a New Jersey tollway! The power of being generous showers kindness on even those we do not know.

The Power to See

Being endowed with limitless light, it seems natural that the *Manipura Chakra* would host the sense of sight. This great gift allows us the ability to see the beauty that surrounds us, the colors of the rainbow as well as the sparkle in our loved ones' eyes.

The eyes, poetically quoted as "the windows of the soul," allow us the ability to view the world. As we look into the eyes of a stranger, we are able to ascertain the world within them. Various emotions show in the eyes—sadness, happiness, fear, anger; all feelings are reflected both outward and inward.

The sense of sight is the most powerful sense. Even if our eyes are closed, hearing a loud noise we open wide. They guide us to pleasant events and warn us of danger. Forming early on in utero, the brain puts forth small buds of brain tissue, which then become our eyes. The eyes feed us external information that is then directly input into the nervous system.

Witnessing a disturbing event, we may see the image and feel it almost at once. A heartwarming event elicits an immediate positive response. "When I first saw her, I knew it was love at first sight." When the moment you first saw her caused your heart to ping, the vision interlaced with the emotions.

The eyes often reveal more than most of us are willing to admit. Better keep those sunglasses handy, in case you are not ready to reveal your inner thoughts and feelings.

The gift of sight is something many of us take for granted. Take time to cherish your eyes for the gifts they give us every day.

Our yearly gifts always include a donation to various

organizations that restore sight to millions of children and adults who have lost the gift of vision through birth defects, malnutrition, or disease. This became a yearly custom since I visited a leper colony in India.

It was something I was looking forward to, a special aspect of India that I had not explored. One of the *Ranis* (queens) had donated a vast piece of land for a rehabilitation center to serve people exposed to and infected by the dreaded disease, leprosy. Not knowing what to expect, but having known about the many horrors of the disease, I still was not prepared for what I saw.

The children were housed and educated separately from their parents but joined together for daily visits. Within the children's housing, there were two sections—one for the children infected with the disease, the other for the ones who were well and not affected by the disease. What a delight it was to visit the different areas. The girls had bows in their hair; the boys wore bright white shirts. Well cared for and with a sense of belonging, the children sang songs they had prepared for us.

We then moved on to the adult region, where people without fingers were weaving beautiful placemats, napkins, shawls, and bedcovers. Their smiles allowed my heart the comfort of knowing they felt useful and productive. The physician in charge came to greet us and, to my surprise, he spoke English with a German accent. His story brought tears to my eyes.

Taking temporary leave from his work as a prominent surgeon in Germany, he had offered his services at the rehabilitation center in India for three months. His idea was to come and train others in a procedure he had developed, which would allow the afflicted to see again. One of the manifestations of leprosy is the progressive inability to open and close the eyelids. When the muscles in the lids atrophy, movement is no longer viable. Seeing becomes impossible, as the window shade is in the closed and locked position.

The seemingly simple procedure (for an expert) took a muscle from the thumb and connected it to the eyelid, allowing it to fulfill its original use. The joyful smiles on the recipients after the procedures were the greatest payment, allowing them to continue to live productive lives.

His passing on the knowledge to other medical professionals allowed more people to be helped. Although he had hoped to put himself out of a job, the need only increased. The three-month stay expanded to ten years. He said it was the happiest ten years of his life.

Long forgotten were the amenities that made life in Germany sweet, along with career hopes and dreams. They were replaced by hundreds of grateful eyes gazing into a bright future.

*Namaste, When I am in the place of love and oneness,
I am empowered and empower others, Namaste.*

A Benevolent Power

When we truly feel powerful, we become aware of the responsibility it bears. It is our duty to protect those more vulnerable. Sadly, in our culture many feel powerless. It seems, then, that the best way to combat the lack of power is to educate us all from an early age that real power comes not from what we do or how many people we control, but from deep within.

A friend was recounting how her very powerful grandfather would enter the board room for a meeting. Having arrived earlier, the board members intentionally left the seat at the head of the table free for the CEO. Often, to make his position clear, the executive would take a center seat at the board table instead. When the protests encouraged him to sit at the head of the table, he retorted, "Anywhere I sit, is the *head* of the table."

As we fortify this power, it congeals and becomes what we experience as charisma. It is a tangible power that radiates confidence. Charisma in itself is neutral; we can use it for good or not. We note that many leaders of the world seem to radiate charisma, making them electable; hopefully it will remain as they govern over the multitudes. But how many can we name who hold that power benevolently? Under that veneer of power, many harbor a deep feeling of inadequacy and powerlessness. The initial presentation to the world appears strong, but once installed the insecurity surfaces, and the abuse of power becomes imminent. The rare times we encounter great leaders whose only interest is the for the good of the people, we are able to hold them in the highest esteem. Two great examples of these leaders are Mahatma Gandhi and Nelson Mandela.

When many think of Mahatma Gandhi, the image emerges of a small man with shaven head, wearing wire glasses and wrapped in a loincloth. Not exactly the picture many of us would formulate as a great leader! While playing, children pretend to be kings and queens, donning elaborate costumes dotted with jewels and furs, forging their power and greatness.

How then can we equate this level of power to a small man sitting on the floor, spinning cotton? Perhaps this is why, in his unassuming way, the great Mahatma was able to bring the entire British Empire to its knees. Quietly disarming, his power was not fostered by jewels, furs, or even a great throne but fortified by the realization that we are one in spirit. His power radiated from justice and truth. Formulating the path he named *Satya Graha*, the path of truth, his inner knowing and conviction directly translated to his outer mission.

One key moment in India's quest for independence came during the salt walks. Denied the right to make their own salt, the nation was obliged to *buy* the salt that was taken from the seas that bordered *their* land. India, experiencing a hot climate much of the year, was completely dependent upon their ever-present need for life-sustaining salt.

The job of manufacturing their own salt seemed to be a natural right. The British Empire, being a foreign power, exerted their dominance by controlling salt production, thereby holding sway over the entire Indian nation.

Realizing that salt was a key component to becoming independent, Gandhi organized a march to the sea. The purpose was to show peaceful non-cooperation by making their own salt. At first the followers were few, but as the dedicated group passed from one village to another, the marching members grew in number.

When at last the sea was in view, the labor of salt-making began. The occupying soldiers, now showing an almost affectionate feeling for the small but mighty man in a loincloth, first tried a gentle approach. Still holding their sticks ready for action, they told him, "Please, Mahatma, turn your group around, otherwise we will need to use force."

Baring his shoulder, Gandhi said, "Please go ahead and

beat me, your superiors are watching. If you do not use your clubs to stop us, you will be punished for forsaking your duty." Even knowing that he and many others would suffer physical abuse and possible imprisonment, his inner strength led him to have kindness and understanding toward his would-be enemy. This sacrifice brought great fruits. Eventually the British succumbed; the salt was manufactured and celebrated by the rightful owners.

The salt walk and the making of salt by and for the Indian community seemed to be one of the major events that eventually "convinced" the British Empire to retreat. They laid their weapons to rest, while withdrawing from the county they had occupied for centuries. India was granted the independence she craved and deserved, to become the mighty nation it is today.

> "Be the light that you want to see in the world." —Mahatma Gandhi

Of all the horrors and injustices in the world, apartheid ranks high on the list. Only a very insecure and powerless group of individuals would reduce another to suffer injustices solely on the basis of skin color.

For those of us living in a "free and democratic" country we may feel complacent and even a bit cocky when we hear the horrors of apartheid. How easily we are able to see the injustices of others in foreign lands. If we delve into our nation's history, we uncover many outrages often supported by the documents our democracy was founded on. Reading carefully through our Charters of Freedom, while giving unalienable rights to some, it declares that those of a particular race are only partially human, bringing glaring injustices to the forefront. As outrageous as it seems to us today, women were not even mentioned in those declarations; they excluded one half of the population of basic rights. Our outrages ring loud and clear for those countries across the world, but when they exist in our own cities, towns and country, we often turn a blind eye.

The induction of apartheid into the South African society was a devastating setback to a civilized society. The mounting inequalities summoned great leaders to be born. Emerging to lead a nation in despair, Nelson Mandela stepped forward. Holding the deep conviction for equality, he organized and rallied the disenfranchised. Also joining the struggle were a growing group of people unaffected by the abuses but fortified with a sense of righteousness for all beings.

After many imprisonments and humiliations, Mandela eventually was convicted of sabotage and conspiracy and sentenced to prison, where he remained for more than twenty-seven years. He continued to fight for equality for all from his jail cell.

When the goal of justice and freedom was finally realized, South Africans held their first multi-racial elections in which full empowerment to all was granted. Nelson Mandela become the first black president of a nation in which *all* were equal. His belief in the benevolent power within raised the consciousness of not just South Africa but the entire world.

*Namaste, When I am in the place of love and oneness,
I am empowered and empower others, Namaste.*

We are now able to understand the great power the *Manipura Chakra* allows us to wield. When used benevolently it manifests as friendship, service, and caring for others. Dominance in this chakra will lead a person with clarity to be a friend to all, honoring others' accomplishments and life choices. It is our responsibility to keep this powerful energy strong and clear.

At this time in history, purifying the *Manipura Chakra* is essential to outweigh the purveyors of malice. With the majority of people wanting peace, our power must carry conviction and have a far-reaching voice, speaking out against injustice, like the greats. In that way, the inner and outer worlds will rejoice in peace and fellowship.

"As I walked out the door toward the gate that would lead to my freedom, I knew if I didn't leave my bitterness and hatred behind, I'd still be in prison." —Nelson Mandela

Breaking Melon With the Enemy

In 1986, travel to the Soviet Union was not recommended on an official level. Travel was *just opening* to American travelers and I was excited about going there to share the benefits of Yoga with any and all who were interested.

After offering numerous lectures and classes to general audiences, I was asked to give a talk about the medical research I was involved in, to a group of military medical personnel. Not exactly sure this was a great decision, I found myself being driven to a military compound some distance outside of Moscow. The long drive so far from the city was making me feel more than a bit uncomfortable. "What if I am imprisoned for some small infraction of the rules? Would anyone know where to find me?" "Oh, yes, I last saw Nischala Devi being taken to a Russian military base somewhere north of here, not sure where!" Not one to let my fears take the driver's seat, I switched to the part of me that was happy to have the adventure.

As I gave my invited presentation, the audience seemed to be riveted to my every word. Afterward, I was invited to have a "special" meeting with the main team of health professionals (all in *powerful* military uniform).

Ushered into a conference room, I realized this was a great honor that few westerners received. In the center of the room a large table loomed, surrounded by chairs occupied by various high-ranking members of the military. For someone of my background, it would have seemed strange to be with the military at all, but adding the detail of being not just in Russia but at a Russian *military installation*, my trepidation loomed large. To dispel any remaining remnant of normalcy, directly in the center of this large board table, sitting all alone, was a gigantic watermelon, one of the largest I had ever seen.

I realized I was about to sit at a table with the great and powerful, but the sight of the watermelon did not allow the seriousness of the moment to launch. Answering many questions, I was intrigued by the command of the English language one of the colonels was exhibiting. I was delighted by the ease with which we were able to communicate. Then casually, perhaps too casually, I asked him where he acquired these impressive language skills. Silence fell upon the room like a heavy blanket dropping from the ceiling.

"Well," he hesitated, "I was in reconnaissance during the war and it was a necessary part of *my job* to know English."

"Oh," I said, smiling, not really understanding that he meant the Cold War with the United States! When the reality of the situation finally sunk in, my whole system went into defense mode. *He*—remembrance rapidly emerging from deep inside my mind—*is the enemy. What do I do now?* The thickness of apprehension began to engulf the essence of good will.

At that moment, an officer appeared with a huge machete. *Now I'm really in trouble!* My mind raced on. Holding firm to my already heightened anxiety, I watched the officer approach the opposite side of the table. I was thankful it was the other side!

Without a moment of hesitation, a skilled and intentional THUD pierced and penetrated the watermelon with gusto. Zapplap! Zapplap! Continuing with the precision of a great surgeon, the fruit was quickly dissected into multiple *huge* pieces. My table partners all donned childlike smiles of anticipation. Watermelon was, at that time, a luxury for the very few and *very* privileged. My visit was the celebrated occasion that created much happiness as they relished this wonderful treat.

Even though I was enjoying them partaking in the treat, I was still a bit uncomfortable about eating this, perhaps, forbidden fruit. I was after all, "breaking melon with the enemy."

Understanding the decorum to share in the bounty, I began to anticipate the tasty treat. While my eyes were searching for the "necessary" plates, and napkins, the Colonel took his half-moon and with great gusto took a big chomp right out of the heart of the melon. He emerged with seeds and juice dripping from his cheeks, nose and chin. To stifle a laugh and not wanting to appear rude, I picked up a sizable piece of watermelon and gingerly took a small bit. On seeing this, my host said, "Not like that, *like this*!" And proceeded to show me how to enjoy the delicacy by immersing his entire face in the crescent.

Coming up for air, he was thoroughly delighted. Without further hesitation, I followed the leader. With seeds, juice and residue everywhere, we both laughed out loud as we dove down for yet another delicious mouthful. The powerful moment did not come from a show of military power, but in the powerful happiness we shared over a common watermelon.

Could the world be a more peaceful and loving place if we put our power into the common good? Perhaps our power could allow us more tolerance and acceptance and maybe, just maybe, we need to share more watermelons!

Namaste, When I am in the place of love and oneness, I am empowered and empower others, Namaste.

Meditation on Manipura Chakra

• • • • •

Allow the body and mind to become quiet.

Feel yourself softening into a deep stillness and peace.

Close the eyes.

Take in a few deep breaths and let them out very slowly.

Begin to venture to the *Manipura Chakra*, at the solar plexus.

There, awaiting your awareness, is a whirling vortex of energy emanating a glowing vibration of yellow color reminiscent of the sun.

This vibration generates outward as the *Manipura Chakra*. It connects us to the force of power and our use of it.

Observe your breath as it flows in and out with ease.

Imagine yourself standing on the earth lifting your face toward the sun.

Stretch your arms and head upward, absorbing the fire element into your body and mind.

Allow it to illuminate your entire being with happiness. (a few moments)

Connecting to the fire element, your power, intellect, and vitality enhances.

Bowing to that vitality, imagine all the greatness you

would be able to accomplish in this world.

Through this dynamic force, you are able to generate energy and vitality. This allows you to live fully and use the clarity of your intellect to learn and explore, accompanied by a high sense of self-esteem.

Feel this dynamic energy attracting happiness.

Welcome the people who support you in your expansion and openness.

Continue to focus your awareness at the *Manipura Chakra* and notice a warmth radiating both inward and outward. (a few moments)

From this center of power, the sense of sight develops, enabling us to see the beauty and gifts of the physical world.

Allow the vision to conjure up a pleasant sight that evokes a sense of happiness. It could be the first flower of spring, a snowfall on a full moon night, a small child's face on Christmas morning.

Notice a smile lighting your face.

Even if you can't recall the scene exactly, the thought will kindle happiness. (One minute)

Become aware as the entire body alights with happiness, tingling with that precious feeling.

Both body and mind become infused with golden yellow, the color of intellect and power.

Allow that vibration and radiance to infuse your entire being. (one minute)

Now invoke the visual image that allows you to recall an event that has caused you to be angry.

Notice how that feels in your body.

Is it the same soothing feeling as the experience of being loved and respected? (a few moments)

Gently allow the unpleasant invocation of anger to transform. Gently invite the delight life holds, back into your consciousness, encircling it with radiant golden light. (a few moments)

Cultivating this ability allows you to shift the mind to the pleasurable when unkindness enters into your world.

Bring the awareness back to the solar plexus.

Recognize the *Manipura Chakra* as a transmitter of energy powered from the internal sun.

Make a silent affirmation to nurture this chakra and the qualities it holds.

It is honored when we honor our own power and use it benevolently.

We then shower the light of love on everyone.

• • • • •

Namaste, When I am in the place of love and oneness, I am empowered and empower others, Namaste.

Chapter Four

Anahatha Chakra

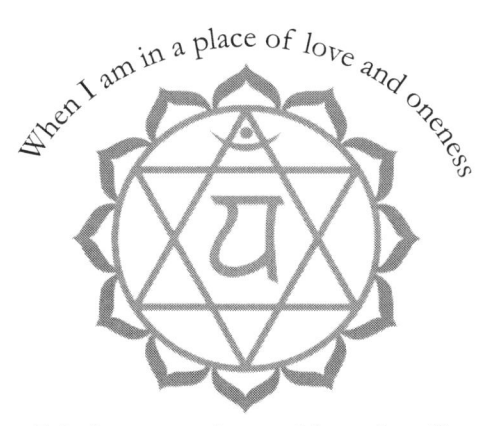

When I am in a place of love and oneness

I feel compassion and love for all

Love and Compassion

A Friend in Need

The phone call unleashed the hidden fear that many of us hold in the recesses of our hearts. This fear is carefully tucked deep in the crevices, deprived of the air required to become real.

For Jan, the fear had unfurled and shattered her heart into tiny pieces. Her beloved husband, away for a quick business trip, encountered a drunk driver head on. The results were unfathomable.

Pushing the momentous shock aside at least momentarily, preparation for travel needed to come first. As if in a daze, she began to ready herself and five small children to fly to a place she had never been—to do a task she never wanted to do.

The children, too young to fully understand, tried to help their distraught mother with the chores. Realizing she was missing some vital articles of clothing necessary for the travel, she left for the store, five small children in tow.

A neighbor a few houses away heard of the tragedy. Wanting to lend comfort and a helping hand, she cautiously approached Jan's house. What could possibly be said or even done? She wondered. Putting her own misgivings aside, she rang the doorbell.

When there was no answer, she quietly tried the door and to her surprise it was unlocked. Cautiously she entered, calling out to announce her presence so as to not cause any more distress.

The stillness of the house alerted her to the fact that the family was out. Not wanting to intrude, she intended to leave when she noticed five pairs of little shoes lined up along the wall, ready for duty. On closer inspection, she saw the shoes were quite dirty and very scuffed, typical of small children's shoes. She smiled and began to walk away.

An idea flashed through her mind. She had come to offer assistance, and this could be her service. Gathering the shoes in a bag, she whisked them away to her home. Searching her closets for polish and a rag, she shined each shoe putting love and compassion in every stroke. Returning the shoes to their rightful place, she went on her way.

Travel completed, the family returned to resume their life, minus one. A few weeks later, Jan saw her neighbor. "Did you come into our home and clean and polish the children's shoes on that tragic day?" A bit shyly the neighbor nodded.

"When I came back from shopping and saw what had been done, I felt like something in the universe was still all right. I had noticed the dirt and scuffs on the children's shoes, but with all I had to do, it was one more thing I could not handle. By that simple act, you showed me that love can be expressed in many ways. Your compassion bolstered me during my darkest time. I am forever grateful and pray that one day I can offer solace to another as you did for me."

> "You have not lived until you have done something for someone who can never repay you." —Anonymous

The Anahatha Chakra

As the energy ascends from the *Manipura* to the *Anahatha Chakra,* we become acutely aware of the major shift in the quality of the attributes. The three earth chakras, *Muladhara, Swadhisthana* and *Manipura,* are under the influence of the *apana-vayu* or downward moving energy. They receive and are nurtured by the earth's energy. Our earthly existence is supported through their elements—earth, water, and fire and the attributes of instinct, passion, and intellect respectively.

Leaping over the great divide between the solar plexus and the heart, we find a dynamic ascending energy enlivening the *Anahatha, Vishudda,* and *Ajna Chakras* that continues to the *Sahasara* and beyond. This refined upward energy allows the *Anahatha* to reflect qualities that represent the more altruistic aspects of our nature.

Exploring the qualities of the *Anahatha Chakra,* we are immediately charmed by its sense of balance and the outpouring of universal love and compassion. Often the *Anahatha Chakra* is simply referred to as the heart chakra, as much for its location as the qualities of love and compassion it holds. Air, being a subtle element, is mutable and while present everywhere is evasive. The element symbolically reminds us that air, like the love within this chakra, cannot be contained, as it saturates even the most minute recesses. We may agree to the properties of air, yet, being intangible, it is often difficult to prove its existence.

Being the first of the Heaven Chakras, we become acutely aware of its positioning—three chakras are below the *Anahatha* and three chakras above. This strategic placement situates the heart chakra at the very center of our being. Its less-than-subtle message clearly conveys: when we live in the heart, our life is in harmony and balance.

As the Earth and the Heaven chakras balance, they appoint the heart as the overseer. Once this happens, all our actions, words, and thoughts are endowed with an overtone of unconditional love.

Imagine a child's pinwheel with two petals and a center disc. When both petals are of equal size they, to everyone's delight, spin. If however, the two petals vary in size the propulsion will differ, not allowing the pinwheel to whirl. This same principle applies to the chakras.

The traditional symbol for the *Anahatha Chakra* is depicted as two intersecting triangles. One points downward and the other upward. The one gesturing down represents the earth, while the upward pointing triangle represents the heavens. The great significance is that the two triangles, seemingly in opposition, intersect to form an entirely new shape and symbol. Instead of the original three-sided triangles, we now have a figure featuring six aspects which are more powerful united than apart.

While all the chakras radiate love, the *Anahatha Chakra* is the eternal source that feeds the others. The shape of the six-pointed star portrays a cosmic diagram of how this function occurs.

While the entire star shape is representative of the *Anahatha Chakra*, at the center of the intersecting triangles the hexagon, with its six open portals, gives us another vision. Directing the wellspring of love through each portal of the hexagon, the six triangles are infused with love and compassion. The triangular shape allows this precious energy to be directed outward. Each triangle then channels that sublime energy to one of the six chakras that it represents, allowing the love to be transformed into the attributes and elements inherent in that chakra.

For example, when this wholehearted love and compassion is channeled into the *Muladhara* or base chakra, it encourages us to love our Mother Earth. While the *Vishudda* or throat chakra is associated with prayer, it is the synergy of love and devotion emanating from the heart that employs the higher communication present in the throat chakra, to create effective and sincere prayer. In this same way, we express love through each of the chakras while the source remains at the heart.

Springtime Green, Loving Pink

The heart chakra vibrates as the color green, the color when spring is born.

It is that soft aura that we experience in the early spring, which gives hope for the future. The color is both soothing and healing. In times before, when faced with a grave illness, people were advised to spend some time in the countryside and sunshine for rest and healing. Trees, those statuesque green giants, do us a great service by producing life-giving oxygen, which we inhale. In turn, we release carbon dioxide as a waste product, which the trees take in as a necessity for their survival.

The green color found in abundance at the countryside is often obliterated by concrete and cement in the cities. To bring vitality to our city lives, we adorn our homes with vibrant plants that live indoors. This allows the radiant color to revitalize us as we bask in the presence of our green friends. Whatever source that energy emanates from, the emerald energy is essential to our health and wellbeing. This is viewed as an act of reciprocal love between plants and humans.

Another way of understanding the equilibrium between the Earth and Heaven Chakras is to recall the color associated with the *Muladhara (base) Chakra* as red, while the *Sahasara (crown) Chakra* is opalescent white. When the three Earth and three Heaven Chakras come into balance the two colors, from opposite polarities, merge. Celebrating this fortunate balance, the color of the heart chakra changes from springtime green to the dazzling pink of love.

Pink represents compassion and love, which is directly associated with the heart on a physical, as well as emotional, level. Often, we would find rose quartz crystals by the hospital bedside of our research participants before and after a procedure. Their vibrant and healing presence soothed all who entered. Wearing a neckless of the pink stone can help expand or soothe the heart physically, emotionally, and spiritually. With the intricate balance of the heaven and earth chakras, the heart chakra radiates an incandescent pink color, filling our aura with love.

A Healing Touch

The sense of touch is associated with the *Anahatha Chakra*. The hands are the servants of the heart, in that as we touch another we are imparting love from our hearts. There are subtle energy channels that allow love and compassion to flow from the heart, down through the arms and into the hands. Many healing modalities from time immemorial employ this simple yet profound way of healing—from a mother's hug when we are scared, to the hand that reaches out to ease our pain.

Most of us are unaware of the presence of healing in

our hands, in our touch. When we observe how a crying baby can be soothed and sedated by simply stroking their soft bellies, this premise is better understood.

Before all the modern drugs and procedures, the country doctor would stay at the bedside of a feverish child, placing cool compresses on the forehead while gently stroking their arms and head. Who can say which method does more healing? Could combining the two double the effect?

The neonatal section of a hospital is a place for rejoicing and a place where dreams can shatter. After a long and arduous labor, two new twin souls, now embodied, joined the earth's family. The cruel news that only one was expected to survive caused deep distress for the once-hopeful parents.

Hospital policy dictated each twin be placed in her own incubator for optimal monitoring and care. The weaker of the two was slipping rapidly, about to return to its cosmic home and out of its newly formed body.

One of the more compassionate nurses caring for the two infants intuitively felt they belonged together in *one* incubator. She reasoned that, for nine months, they had cleaved to each other as escorts through their journey toward birth. Why separate them now, when the one so desperately needed her sister's love and companionship?

Disobeying hospital protocol, she took the stronger of the two and placed her in the same bed with her sister. The welcome was astonishing to those watching. When the weaker of the two was placed next to her womb-mate, the stronger one, with great compassion and love, raised her arm up and placed it around her sister's shoulders. They were locked in an embrace. For newborns, the movement

of lifting the arm high up and placing it over the
of another was thought to be an impossible feat. B
it with their tearing eyes, the team nodded at the m..cle.

The greatest part of the miracle had yet to come. As the twins embraced one another, the weaker infant's vital signs began to normalize. The doctors were able to decree that the weaker twin would share a full and normal life with her loving sister. Both twins would thrive, and it was a loving touch that healed.

*Namaste, When I am in the place of love and oneness,
I feel compassion and love for all, Namaste.*

Because we have now traversed the boundaries into the Heaven Chakras, we recognize a subtler aspect of the sense of touch, *clairsentience*. This subtle sense allows us to *feel* that which is intangible and elusive. It brings clear knowledge of thoughts, events, actions, even dangers, where no obvious substance to the claims could be found. Many of us have this natural ability, but with mothers and their children it seems most apparent. Referred to often as a sixth sense, most parents will "feel" what is happening with their children, even when thousands of miles away. Conversely, babies can sense when their mother is distressed or happy, and become cranky or happy themselves, mirroring the mother's feelings. We all have the ability to access this *clairsentience;* however, how much we trust it determines whether it strengthens or weakens.

The *Anahatha Chakra* holds intuition as part of its power, a connection to the subtle realm that speaks to each of us from a place that is well beyond the cognitive mind's reach. Once seen as an evil force, it is now touted as a coveted gift of a few. For women, intuition is so inherent that it is often termed *Woman's Intuition*. Yet, for millennia, few women were honored or rewarded for these gifts. Most were punished and persecuted or even burned at the stake for reaching into the subtle realms to offer truths. Regardless of the consequences, ordinary women as well as saints were lifted from the mundane and elevated to the mystical by the ability to "feel" what the future would bring and preventing possible danger.

In current times people, known as intuitives, comfortably use this extraordinary sense of perception to diagnose medical conditions. They are also recruited by law enforcement and reconnaissance to predict and apprehend the wrongdoers. All of this occurs because of the *Anahatha Chakra* and the intuition it embraces.

"Intuition is more important than intellect."
—Albert Einstein

Healing From the Heart

To many of us who have health issues, the concept of healing becomes paramount. We yearn to be brought back to wholeness, so life can be enjoyed to the fullest. Hearing the terms healing versus curing, we are often confused. Curing implies that we are already ill and are in need of something or someone to make us well. Healing is coaxing the body, mind, spirit back into harmony through healthful means, thereby affecting a return to wholeness.

In our effort to be self-determining and successful in the world, we may inadvertently do harm to the body by over-indulging in work, food, or addictive substances. Also, in the process, we isolate ourselves from our true nature, each other, and our Mother Earth. Healing happens when we sow and reap love, holding others in the highest respect.

Our bodies require much care. We spend many hours a day feeding and grooming, all in hopes of reaping vitality and enhancing our overall appearance. We are coaxed to eat healthy food, take vitamins, exercise, and visit a health practitioner when needed, ensuring us a strong chance of maintaining radiant health. In this way, we can say we are giving love to the body.

We must also treat our minds with similar watchfulness. We allocate a great deal of time to learning new information, finding ways to keep the mind alert and vital, while anticipating the ongoing challenge of getting along with others. We know a clear mind can help further our career and make life interesting and dynamic.

But how many of us pay concentrated attention to our hearts? Do we utilize the unlimited ability of the heart to love and cherish one another unconditionally?

As infants, we arrive openhearted and loving. Eyes wide open, we accept everyone as an aspect of ourselves. As we welcome all into our hearts, we smile. Touching that loving place in others, they are instantly drawn in to our hearts—we are one!

This recognition of the Divine in all has the ability to sustain us through our entire lifetime. When our heart blossoms, if we invite it to take the lead in our lives, the mind is relegated to follow. Seems to be opposite of how, much of the time, the heart is recruited only on special occasions.

When put on first response, the heart and the love that it holds becomes the chief advisor when faced with a sweet or difficult issue. If we constantly choose the path of analysis and observation over love and compassion, before long the oneness in the heart becomes shrouded by the discriminating mind. The unity has taken a step back into the shadows. To retain the openness, allow the heart to lead, with the mind and intellect taking a close second place, to create and encourage balance and harmony.

Please understand that the love that is represented by the *Anahatha Chakra* is not the ordinary love of romantic tales and fantasies. The usage of the word *Love* has become a catch word for anything we like.

Can the love for our car, our house, our hair be the same as loving our children, partners, parents, neighbors? The love that radiates in this chakra holds the qualities of totality, unconditional and wholehearted. Many of the ways we express love mentioned above are conditional, based on time, circumstances and mood.

To love someone wholeheartedly means that any changes that occur with them or you are never a critical enough reason to withdraw your caring. It is interesting that the traditional wedding vows seem to understand this. Each couple is asked to pledge their love to each other in front of witnesses. They solemnly renounce the pair of opposites that have the potential to cause love to fade. *In sickness and in health*—how easy to be with someone when they are hale and hearty, how difficult to care for someone when they have fallen ill. *For richer or poorer*—celebrating love for each other even when the only financial option is to toast your love with tap water.

At a friend's wedding, I overheard the groom give a conditional compliment followed by an ultimatum to the bride. "You look magnificent today. Your beauty is radiant. Make sure you always look like you do today." Not exactly what the wedding vows intended to convey. He asked the impossible; we, as part of nature, change constantly. We are not even the same as we were yesterday. How could she look the same in 5, 10 or 20 years? If their love for each other deepens, she will be even more beautiful to him as the years take her youth, replacing it with inner radiance. We need to love with our whole heart, unconditionally, for better *or* worse.

We often see the truth of this enduring love in couples who have sustained bitter hardships while remaining firmly rooted to their love for each other. A difficult situation, such as the loss of a child or an illness, will test the underpinnings of enduring love. How a couple handles these situations tests and portrays the strength of their true love.

On one of our Cancer Retreats, I became close to a couple married fifty years; he still called her his "bride." His health was in rapid decline and the unfathomable sorrow of parting after a lifetime of love was cloaked and hidden, too painful to be in the open. After the retreat, we vowed to keep in contact; my heart was with them in their joy *and* sorrow.

A call for counsel came a few weeks later. It was the "bride" calling, desperation in her voice. Her sweetheart had taken a turn for the worse, and she was frustrated and felt ineffectual in helping relieve his unsurmountable pain. Feeling her distress, my heart enveloped her with compassion.

She spoke until weeping obliterated her words. Assessing the situation, it was clear that she was in need of as much attention as her ailing "groom."

"Is there someone at the house helping to care for him?" I asked.

"Oh, yes," she said. "We have someone full time and lots of help popping in from time to time."

"Do you feel confident that they are able to take good care of him?"

"Yes, of course, they are professionals and know exactly what to do to keep him comfortable."

"Okay then, I think the best thing for you to do now, both for you and for him, is to go to the theater and see a happy movie."

Not believing what she was hearing, she asked, "You want me to leave my sick husband and go to a movie?"

"That's right."

"When should I do that?"

"As soon as possible. Look for a cheerful movie nearby and go."

Feeling that I had caused her to doubt my sanity, we parted phone company.

The next day we were back on the phone.

"When you said to go to the movies yesterday, I felt you might have somehow missed the gravity of the situation. Hanging up the phone, I told my husband what you said. Expecting him to agree with my observation, he laughed and handed me the car keys. 'Go,' he said, 'it will be good for your wellbeing as well as mine. I am being well taken care of, but no one is taking care of you. My heart will be happy knowing that you have had at least a couple of hours of lightness and levity in the midst of this long illness that is taking my body away from you.'"

So off she went. Upon her return she was able to share the lightness of the storyline with him as if he had been there. Together they shared their thoughts and impressions of the movie, reinforcing their enduring love.

Namaste, When I am in the place of love and oneness, I feel compassion and love for all, Namaste.

Could sharing love and recognizing that we are one be a way of healing strife with friends, family, governments, countries and our Mother Earth? Could it be that simple?

In an effort to understand what makes us sick and what makes us well, many scientific studies have been conducted. Some are large, with many aspects and volunteers, others are smaller, with fewer participants.

It would not occur to most of us to think that a light touch of the hand could change the rate of recovery or elicit good tips, but in this controlled study that is exactly what happened.

In a busy general hospital, nurses were instructed to follow a new protocol. If the room they were entering was on the right side of the hallway, when dispensing medication they were to place the pills on the bedside table. For the rooms on the left side of the hall, they were to hand the medication directly, making sure that the patient received a gentle touch along with the meds. This was then observed and charted. When the data was analyzed, the results caused surprise and delight.

The patients lucky enough to be in the rooms where they were briefly touched before taking medication recovered quicker, with fewer complications, and were discharged from the hospital earlier than their counterparts. All from a simple touch from one heart, to the hands, to the other heart.

Someone thought to try this same study in completely different setting. Wait staff in a busy restaurant were told that for the customers seated on the right side of the restaurant, when presenting the bill place it on the table, making certain not to touch anyone. For the left side of the restaurant, they were instructed to lightly brush against the patron's shoulder or if appropriate touch their arm.

Whether the gentle touch was consciously felt or not customers, unaware of the reason, started to tip more than those not touched. Regardless of the yummy food consumed, we are starving for touch and are willing to leave a large tip for that affection.

Namaste, When I am in the place of love and oneness, I feel compassion and love for all, Namaste.

Seva, Selfless Service

Understanding that we all have a great capacity for wholehearted love, how can it be expressed in everyday life? Many of us could agree that certain people naturally express this great gift by shining their love on everyone. For the rest of us, constant focus may be needed.

Where we choose to sprinkle our love is often in places of agreement or people who share our same views, opinions, family of origin, or even a sports team. We use love as a commodity which we dole out sparingly or in abundance according to our ideals. The heart, being like a revolving door, swings inward to welcome love sent our way, opening out to set it free to light on a loving target. The wider it swings open, the larger the opening to allow the love to return.

The majority of people seem to be generous expressing love with those they know but stingy with strangers. Many of the difficulties in this world come because we are constantly screening and assessing which direction our love should flow. What would the world be like if, instead of looking at differences between ourselves and others, we focused on the light shining brightly in each heart? We seem to all want the same things—health, prosperity, safety, and LOVE. Why can we not hold that truth higher than the dualistic aspects of 'like' and 'dislike'?

Included among the spiritual practices of most traditions of the world is performing service to those less fortunate. The Sanskrit word *Seva* means to perform service with an open heart and attitude, so both the server and the one served are enriched by being with each other. Another term used is *Karma Yoga*, *Karma* meaning action or purification and *Yoga*, meaning union. Putting the words together, we learn that we can reach union with the Divine through our loving actions. It is considered by many as one of the highest forms of spiritual practice. Sitting quietly in prayer or meditation is a sublime practice between you and your inner self. While sitting with your own mind can be challenging, it could become the practice of choice when confronted with serving a grumpy stranger. The temptation to walk away, leaving the service behind, would be a viable lure. *Seva* seems to be one of the simplest and quickest ways to open a heart to love and compassion.

When we serve another, a deeper understanding of who they really are surfaces. Often, we are charmed by the depth of their character, sometimes shocked by their deeds. Whatever the experience, it is we who benefit much more from the service. If we can adopt the attitude that the person we are feeding, reading to, dressing is helping us purify our hearts, the act is complete. It is important to bring the heart into the attitude of service, not just the physical action.

As a child, when we would come across someone in great need, my compassionate mother would always quote: "There but for the grace of God go I." After hearing it for many years my young heart learned to bring forth love and compassion where the mind wanted to interject judgement. With years of spiritual practice the phrase evolved. "There but for the grace of God go I" became "There go I." We are One.

Compassion is a sacred concept that is often confused with pity. While we read about the saints who exhibited compassion, the common reaction we often employ to unpleasant situations is judgement or pity. Two difficult options, neither allowing the heart to stay open.

The word *com-passion* means to be *with* someone in pain or distress. It doesn't include pity or even taking on their pain; it is a way of being present. A soothing presence will invite unfettered self-expression, and if we trust in our hearts judgement will not follow.

Service can take place in many forms: feeding the homeless, reading to the sick, taking clothes to a charity. Find what is comfortable for you and slowly, as your heart expands, expand your service as well.

Living in the United States, one of the wealthiest countries in the world, it is sad to see so many people without a place to lay their heads or food to fill their stomachs. Can you pass someone on the street in need without closing your heart as you continue on your way? When they ask for food, how does it make you feel? Do you, can you, turn away?

My friends, being great devotees of Saint Francis of Assisi, honored his memory by spending Friday afternoons making sandwiches and serving them to the homeless on Saturday morning. This became not only their routine but their spiritual practice. Wanting to share the great joy of *Seva*, they enlisted the help of teenage children in an exclusive private school. When the headmistress was approached with the idea, she was so delighted to have the students take part in this great service on Friday afternoons, that she enriched the *Seva* to include going to the shelter on Saturday to feed the people directly.

Politicians, often misguided, tend to neglect the people they were elected to serve. A law was invoked forbidding anyone but city officials to feed the homeless. If the city did it in the first place, we the citizens would not have to do it. But that logic was lost in the shuffling of bureaucratic red tape.

Distressed by the news, the sandwich makers made another visit to the school. Listening very intently, the principal shook her head. "We cannot allow politics to stand in the way of serving those in need. I have an idea. Most of the children in this school come from privileged families. One mother I am thinking of is an anchor for the six o'clock news. My guess is she will be very interested in this story.

Well before you could say *find a shelter*, my friends had a warm, dry building and a dedicated parking space for their van brimming with food.

It was a rainy Saturday morning, and in a moment of enthusiasm I had volunteered to accompany my friend on the weekly ritual. Reluctant to leave my warm and cozy house, I overrode my mind's protests and followed my heart's call. Sloshing down the highway, windshield wipers in full arches, I was on my way with sandwiches and hot drinks in tow.

Approaching the shelter, my mood skyrocketed to gratitude. There for several city blocks was a line of soggy wet people waiting for a sandwich and a hot drink, the same ones I was bringing. My crankiness retreating to ancient history, I unloaded the food and placed it on the long tables. Expecting to hear complaints and grouchy sounds from the now very wet and hungry group, my heart lightened to see them smile.

My *Seva* on this particular morning was to hand out corn chips and I felt very generous at that moment. Giving a hefty portion to one man, I was startled by his response. Stepping back from the table, he thrust his hands in the air and in a booming voice said, "God, I want you to bless this woman for coming out in this weather to serve food to all of us." And turning his attention to me, he said, "God is blessing you." Stunned, my hand holding the chips ready to be delivered dropped. He was blessing me? I should be the one honoring *him*. I had a wonderful warm and dry home, he lived on the streets. I was deeply humbled.

After the last person in line had been served my friend said there was more food to distribute, so we were moving to a different, slightly illegal, location. Loading the food back in the van, off we went to a local park. On approach, we faced a square devoid of people. I was thinking that the rain kept everyone inside, then I remembered that they did not have an *inside*. My friend in a loud voice yelled FOOD and more than 30 people appeared, seemingly out of nowhere.

While we were putting the food out, I noticed the Saint Francis devotee, speaking very animatedly to a woman in a hoodie. Keeping to the task at hand, I paid little attention until she approached me directly. Not stopping my duty of putting out the food, I noticed she came closer. "Stop what you are doing," she said. I tried to disregard her. "You cannot feed these people." Whirling, my mind tried to understand what was happening. I remained silent. "Do you understand me? You cannot give these people food."

My not speaking led her to believe that I did not understand English. She began again in Spanish, this time flashing a very shiny police badge. Digesting this new information, it seemed like a good time to speak. "I hear what you are saying, but it is very difficult for me to understand you. We have food, these people are hungry, it seems like a perfect match!"

"You are breaking the law; if you do not leave, I will have to arrest you." For a long moment I considered being arrested to make a statement. But remembering how cold a jail cell can get at that time of year, I chose another route. Looking into the officer's eyes I asked, "What can we do to help these people? I know you are a good person and care about them. Let's figure out how to serve them."

Her mind, or was it her heart, searched for a solution; after a time she offered, "Okay, you can leave the food, but you cannot serve them personally." A compromise I could embrace.

As we finished putting out the food, a few of the diners rushed to grab whole packs of muffins as well as other food. One of the leaders, shouted, "Brothers and sisters let's not be greedy. If we take only as much as we need, all will have food. But first, we must give thanks." For the second time that day, I witnessed hands becoming airborne as they began. "Almighty God, we are asking you to bless these people for coming out today in this weather to serve us food. Please protect them so they can continue to serve." They then came in single file to take food for *their need but not their greed.*

The rain was getting heavier as we piled back in the van. The windshield wipers on full seemed to be unable to clear the view. Realizing the windshield was in fact clear, the mist that I saw was caused by my eyes, filled with tears.

Maya Angelou's beautiful quote seems sum it up:

"The elderly whose pillows we plumped or whose water pitchers we refill may or may not thank us for our gift, but the gift is upholding the foundation of the universe. Children to whom we read simple stories may or may not show gratitude, but each boon we give strengthens the pillars of the world."
—Maya Angelou

Namaste, When I am in the place of love and oneness, I feel compassion and love for all, Namaste.

I Give You My Heart

There are as many ways to serve as there are hearts with the desire to be of service. In these modern times, a new way to share your heart with others has manifested. There are a precious few who have the ability to offer a life-altering solution, when their own life is forfeited, perhaps at too young an age.

Organ transplants have been available for some years now and, for many who are in need, this is literally the gift of life. Of all the parts and organs that can be transplanted from one person to another, the physical heart seems to offer the most complexities.

Most of us realize that our bodies indeed have an expiration date, but we lack the ability to decipher the actual time! As we live longer and harder, while we function well as a whole, it seems some of our parts start to wear out.

The physical heart miraculously can now be transplanted into another's body, someone who would otherwise cease to live due to the malfunctioning pump. While many organs are now viable for transplant—the liver, kidney, lung, etcetera—the only one so far reported to have mystical "side effects" is the heart.

Organ donors must decide in advance if they are interested in donating, often by putting the words *Organ Donor* on their driver's license. The donation can be anything from a cornea to a heart and all the parts in between. Often, hearts are donated from those who have died in an accident. The heart, usually harvested in another city or state, is packed in ice and shipped by air. The next person on the transplant list is the lucky recipient. The surgical team is on alert and as soon as the heart arrives, the organ is replanted giving a new lease on life to the recipient. Sometimes changes occur that are not always physical in nature.

I received a call one morning from a dear friend who was chief of cardiology at a large teaching hospital. It seems they were performing successful heart transplants and some unusual "memories" and "dreams" were occurring.

One man, in particular, spooked my friend to the point that he called me for another perspective. The patient had a congenital heart defect that did not seriously affect him until later in life. By 50, he needed to have a heart transplant or his life would end. His disability hampered his capacity to work, play, and interact with family and friends.

On the transplant list for a year, his hopes dwindled as the days passed.

On the day he received the call, he was unable to get out of bed due to great weakness and pain. Yet, his spirits soared! With the operation a success and rehabilitation complete, he was ready to start his life anew.

Relieved of years of cardiac symptoms, the transplant now seemed to conjure up a peculiar effect arising not from the physical but from the emotional or even spiritual heart. Because of his physical restriction for many years, he had learned to do quiet things—reading, board games, cards—avoiding sports or other outdoor fun adventures.

Soon after his physical recovery, he started having a vivid and very telling dream. This reoccurring dream encouraged him to begin to partake in more outward activities, plus it kept emphasizing it had *one specific request*. One of the main sources for organ donors are motorcycle accidents. The donor is often of a younger age and the death, while tragic, is often not fraught with long term pain and suffering. With great sadness, the relatives of the donor affirm the request. While the transplant recipient is not given any personal information about the donor, the "dreams" often reveal the specifics.

In this particular case, my friend's patient came to him with this "dream."

"I would like medical clearance to fly to another state," he requested.

"What for?"

"I am having this reoccurring dream that is coming more frequently and I know if I do not fulfill its request, it will continue to haunt me. In the dream, the man whose heart now beats in my chest comes to me. I can see him very clearly. He wears a black leather jacket and a helmet. He is requesting that I go to this specific city and tell his parents that I have his heart, and that he is in a good place, peaceful and happy. He regrets being unable to say goodbye, and most of all he wants me to tell them that he loves them very much." The address and description of the house, the parents, and even where his photo was displayed were included in his vision.

A bit stunned, his doctor gave the permission needed for travel. When the mission was completed the heart transplant recipient returned to a renewed life, made possible through the kindness of a man with a wonderful heart. It seems the motorcycle rider also moved on to a better place; as soon as the request was fulfilled, the "dreams" ceased.

All the stories may not be as dramatic, but it seems even if not reported, the heart retains some essential fragments from the previous owner. Can you imagine the family's surprise when a complete stranger knocks on their door and says, "I have your son's heart! He was 6'3" and wore a blue shirt and black leather jacket the day he died." And they're saying "Yes, yes!" This is not a reality show, it's really happening.

Being fascinated by this whole concept of what the heart holds in its fiber, it seemed likely I would have experienced interesting encounters. This time it was in a hospital waiting room.

Anticipating a loved one's return from surgery is always nerve-racking as the mind ricochets from the best to the worst scenarios. Waiting a bit impatiently for my father-in-law to return from the operating room, I noticed a man sitting by himself.

It seemed like a great distraction for me and I thought he could use someone to talk to. A wonderful time for *karma yoga*. Gently, I went up to him and asked if I could join him. He shyly nodded his head. Taking a seat, I asked him who he was waiting for.

"My wife is having open heart surgery."

"Are you frightened?"

"Yes, very," he added. I started to explain about the procedure, but he politely stopped me, and said he knew it well as he had the same surgery a few years back. Since his surgery was not successful, he subsequently needed to have a heart transplant. My ears perked up hearing this. Cautiously I asked if he had had anything unusual occur on a mental, emotional level after the transplant surgery. His shifting physical position told me volumes.

"Would you like to tell me what happened?" I asked as softly as I could.

"It is really silly," he said, "I have not told anyone."

"It might be good to share it."

He began, "When I was still in recovery, I started to

write poems. At first I did not realize what I was doing as I had never read, let alone written, poetry in my life. One after another they started to pour out of me. I was barely able to write them down. They seemed to be aiding my healing process. The more they came, the stronger I felt. It went on for a long time, but after a while it stopped. I kept them all. Now I am told that the transplant is failing, the chest pain has returned along with shortness of breath."

My heart was reacting as I listened. With his last declaration an intuitive thought arose in me. "Did you ever have the idea that re-reading them could help you return to health?" Something I said triggered a response. He picked his head up, and with bright sparkling eyes he whispered, "I thought the very same thing, but it seemed farfetched. Now that you are saying it too, I will bring them out again to read and recite them. Perhaps I will even be able to write poetry again. And maybe, just maybe, my heart will heal."

Some religions do not allow organs or blood transferred from one person to another. They believe that it affects the donor as well as the recipient and that a subtle part of each individual lives in the blood or tissue. Because of these "paranormal" experiences, even the scientific community is realizing that vital aspects of us can actually be transferred from one being to another, and that our vital essence lives in the human heart!

Namaste, When I am in the place of love and oneness, I feel compassion and love for all, Namaste.

A Humble Example

No matter how clear and good our intention, with our very busy and full lives, the idea of committing time each week for *Seva* may seem unrealistic. We then hold in high esteem those who dedicate their lives to full time service to others. Those who have taken religious vows garner higher expectations for performing selfless service. When we hear of their *Seva* and accomplishments our hearts rejoice.

Saint Teresa of Calcutta, formerly known as Mother Teresa of Calcutta, has been an inspiration to me for a long time. Her strength and vision allowed her to accomplish great feats, which the average person could only imagine. Many of us are unable to keep a dry eye when hearing of Teresa freeing a dying person stuck to the road by their dried body excretions and embracing them in her arms moments before death arrives. They are given assurance through action that they are loved, even as they transition to other worlds.

One of my favorite stories of Saint Teresa exhibits clearly her compassion, strength, and love for all. Mother Teresa was in Beirut when she learned that an orphanage housing many children, deep in war torn territory, was hit by a bomb that knocked out the water supply and the road. No regular cars or vans could pass. Mother Teresa tried to send water and food, but the old rickety van was unable to surmount the rugged passes.

She was trying in vain to convince army officials and diplomats to allow her to go behind enemy lines and escort children to safety. The consensus of head-shaking revealed their vehement disapproval. Their mistake was to underestimate this small, yet dynamic woman. "This is a life-threatening situation for the children. They are without food or water. What would need to take place for me to bring the children to safety?" She continued her questioning, ignoring the snickers.

"It would take a miracle, a complete cease fire, to be able to rescue those children."

A miracle? That was a word she knew something about. "Okay, let's us pray for that miracle." Folding her hands she closed her eyes and began to pray. The officials, embarrassed to be praying at a negotiating table, joined in halfheartedly.

She must have had a direct line to the Divine, because the next thing they knew the cease fire had happened, and off she went to save the grateful children!

My reverence for this great woman only grew through the years, hearing of her courage and one-pointed dedication. That is why my heart rejoiced during an encounter, in an underground cave, with a few great souls filled with light and love.

In the high mountains above the glistening Adriatic, I was descending into the womb of Mother Earth. This particular cavern was scattered with stalactites and stalagmites, pillars of golden formations attesting to the passage of time and perfection of Mother Nature.

Traveling with me through this miraculous beauty was a cluster of nuns from the order founded by Saint Teresa of Calcutta. Vowed to serve the poorest of the poor, they are permitted only two days a year for a holiday outing. This was one of those two precious days.

Moving through this astonishing phenomenon of nature, I experienced a deep sense of awe and humility at the spectacular formations. My companions, the humble nuns, along with the crystals, stirred a deep respect in my heart. How they were able to perform their demanding service with such open and compassionate hearts was inspiring *and* curious to me.

I offered my thanks to them for their continuous service. "It is a privilege to do this service," one of them replied. "But not always easy. Our founder, Saint Teresa was able to show us a tireless example of service, which we strive to emulate daily."

"What was she like?" I asked.

Drawing inward for a brief moment, the nun replied. "She was so many things—strong, determined, dedicated, kind, compassionate. But to me, her shining glory was her great humility. Never for one moment did she think it was she doing it. She offered every bit of good that she did to the divine orchestrator of all good deeds."

My eyes misted with this revelation. As the tour ended we hugged each other. Not letting go, my new friend had a specific request. With sparkling eyes she spoke, "It is a privilege to do this service. I only hope I can one day be as humble as our great fearless founder." She then asked my name. When I told her, she added, "Please pray for us that we may always remember what a privilege it is to serve the poorest of the poor."

> "The miracle is not that we do this service, the real miracle is that we LOVE to do this service." —Saint Teresa of Calcutta

Namaste, When I am in the place of love and oneness, I feel compassion and love for all, Namaste.

Meditation on the Anahatha Chakra

• • • • •

Allow the body and mind to become quiet.

Feel yourself softening into a deep stillness and peace.

Close the eyes.

Take in a few deep breaths and let them out very slowly.

Bring the awareness to the Heart Center.

There, awaiting your awareness, is a whirling vortex of energy emitting a glowing vibration of soft green color, reminiscent of the early spring.

This vibration generates outward as the *Anahatha Chakra*. It connects us to the forces of intuition, love, and compassion.

Observe your breath as it flows in and out with ease.

Bring your focus to the very center of your heart, where Divine Love resides.

Observe when the heart beats, love flows outward.

As the heart rests, love flows back to the heart. (a few moments)

With each inhalation, observe the love in the heart deepening.

On the exhalation, allow that love to flow outward.

Continue to breathe deeply as you observe the love in

the heart expanding to become the size of the heart itself. (a few moments)

Inhale, observe the love as it expands to fill the entire body. (a few moments)

Exhale, send that love out to someone who may need that loving energy.

As you inhale, the love deepens and on the exhale, surround them with this love.
If there is a message to accompany this love, send it silently now. (a few moments)

As you inhale, continue to access the love in your heart.

On the exhalation, allow that love to fill the entire room.

Inhale, the love deepens.

Exhale, it flows outward as love.

Allow the love to continue to expand beyond the room to embrace each flower, tree, and plant on Mother Earth. (one minute)

Continue to expand the love in your heart to all the animals. (a few moments)

Expand that love to all human beings, in every land in this world. (a few moments)

Let your love fill the streams, lakes, rivers, and oceans until it merges with the very core of our Mother Earth.

Absorbing this love offering, Gaia offers this healing energy to all, soothing the entire world. (one minute)

From this deep place of love and compassion, choose an affirmation that encourages you to share love with all, unconditionally. Use it daily or anytime you wish to initiate a heart opening. (one minute)

Slowly and gently begin to bring the awareness back to your own heart, the origin of this love.

Honor it as a source for universal love and compassion.

As all love flows from an eternal source, it greatly amplifies when shared.

The oneness is complete!

● ● ● ● ●

Namaste, When I am in the place of love and oneness, I feel compassion and love for all, Namaste.

Chapter Five

Vishudda Chakra

When I am in a place of love and oneness

I understand everything

Understanding and Higher Communication

Singing to the Divine

The sun streaming through the stained glass windows cast a rainbow onto the altar of a grand church on a warm Sunday morning. Madeline, an older parishioner, was trying to steady herself as she dressed for her solo.

The congregation was settling in as the minister was approached by a famous opera singer, offering to perform at the service. Accepting the generous offer, the minister in his delight neglected to tell Madeline that the 23rd Psalm she had arranged to perform would also be sung by the virtuoso.

With much fanfare, the celebrity was introduced and struck a poised position on stage. Beginning his rendition, the congregation moved into rapture. With the final bow, the audience leapt to their feet and cheered *bravo! bravo!* as he dramatically left the stage.

The minister, assuming that Madeline would relinquish her performance, quickly mentioned her name stating that she had planned to also offer the 23rd Psalm in song. Expecting Madeline to graciously bow out, he started to move on to a different hymn.

Not to be deterred, as her name was mentioned, Madeline slowly rose out of the pew and hobbled down the aisle to the podium. All eyes were on her as she cautiously climbed the few steps. Settling in at center stage, she cleared her throat and began to sing. The smoothness of her predecessor was replaced with a raspiness and an occasional crackling of her voice. Unfazed, she continued. The prayer completed, she slowly began her descent down the steps and hobbled up the aisle, returning to her seat. In the congregation not a sound could be heard, not even a whisper nor a cough. It was as if the entire church plunged into deep prayer.

Later, the opera singer was interviewed about the contrast of reactions to his and Madeline's singing, how his rendition brought cheers and bravos, while the unpolished version evoked a sense of complete silence.

What could be the reason for the two opposite reactions?

"I spent many years training my voice, plus the strict daily practice to become the singer I am today. I am a professional who performed an excellent rendition of the 23rd Psalm. The reaction I received would be expected. The old lady had none of that training, but from the reaction of the group, it was clear she *knew the Lord*!

Let the heart speak through the center of highest communication; as the *Anahatha Chakra* emanates love, the *Vishudda Chakra* has the capacity to express it.

The Vishudda Chakra

As the energy ascends from the *Anahatha Chakra*, we discover the ever-so-subtle *Vishudda (throat) Chakra* manifesting the rarified ether element that propels us beyond the earth's jurisdiction to the infinite blue of the sky. This subtle essence allows us to discern and understand sounds, gifting us with the sense of hearing, speech, and the ability to understand that which the ordinary mind cannot.

The elements attributed to the Heaven Chakras of which the *Vishudda Chakra* is counted, are much subtler than those that comprise the Earth Chakras. Being the subtlest of the earth's elements, ether's aspect is revealed as *prana*. *Prana* is the elusive ever-present universal life force that asks us to take a leap of faith through understanding. It permeates and inhabits the natural world, infusing every cell of our physical body with this universal energy field. Different traditions honor it by different names, *prana* by the Yogis, *qi* by the Japanese and *chi* by the Chinese. Even as the names vary, the universal consensus is that it is the most vital component of life.

The amount of circulating *prana* varies from person to person, day to day, and often moment to moment. At times, for a variety of reasons, there seems to be more or less available *prana*, but while the quantity may fluctuate, the purity does not. The days when we have overspent our *prana* through doing too much—work, eating, even playing—we experience it as fatigue. We even use the expression, "I have no energy today." The ebb and flow of energy is natural; when balanced and steady, it is available for physical, mental, emotional, and spiritual pursuits.

Prana is present in plants, trees, animals, as well as

humans, infusing all with vital life force. Essential *prana* is present in each of the five elements and can be imbued by walking barefoot on the earth, cleansing with water, basking in the sun, inhaling pure air. Our senses also play a vital role in augmenting the already-circulating *prana*: through the beauty we see, the sounds we hear, the touch we receive, the fragrance we smell, the food we eat, and of course the love we embrace. The sun, the moon, the stars, thoughts, actions, and words all have the capacity to enhance or diminish *prana*.

Prana secures our body's health through proper digestion of food, warding off diseases, and fostering an all-over sense of wellbeing. Essential to our survival, the clearer and stronger the life force, the better we look, feel and act.

When the *prana* becomes clear and steady, mental decisions are easier, the emotions find their rightful place, and a renewed fulfillment is experienced even in the smallest things we do. Life can sail along at a smoother pace with fewer bumps and valleys when the vital life force is balanced.

As we are at once spirit *and* nature, the intelligent prana flows to whichever aspect beckons for fulfilment. If taking a long hike, *prana* will be recruited to supply physical energy. If meditating, chanting, or praying the *prana* will be summoned to take us to great heights.

Nature in Her wisdom gives us a great example that occurs annually. A tree in winter has less circulating *prana* than a tree in the springtime. In winter, the sap is withdrawn into the trunk and roots; it is often difficult to convince ourselves that with the promise of spring the life force will enliven the tree and fullness will be restored. The *Prana* flows freely in springtime, as maximum energy is needed for the tree to sprout leaves and flower. *Prana* is the cosmic intelligence that responds to varying needs, including restoring life to a dormant tree. As the leaves and branches draw warmth from the sun and the roots are infused with precious water, the entire tree is nourished with this vital life force. *Prana* is similar to electricity in that it supplies an invisible current to keep life flowing and functioning.

Namaste, When I am in the place of love and oneness, I understand everything, Namaste.

The strategic location of the *Vishudda Chakra* at the throat is the junction between the heart and head (mind). A benevolent effect occurs when the two are in alignment, but disharmony occurs when the two are conflicted. Challenged with an opposing decision, the heart may suggest compassion while the head (mind) is assessing the logical action. The result is confusion and, therefore, a hindrance of energy in the *Vishudda Chakra*.

Unlike the three Earth Chakras which are ever-present and available to function from the birth of our existence on this earth, the Heaven Chakras, and *Vishudda* in particular, release energy in measured proportions. When the Earth Chakras align, the vital energy is encouraged to migrate upward, encouraging the release of greater quantities of this rarified *prana* from the *Vishudda Chakra*. With this infusion of energy, the Heaven Chakras are activated and become beacons that guide our lives.

The *Throat Chakra* has in its control the perception of time. When the energy descends from the heavens, time is activated; if ascending from the earth centers, we cease to be limited by time. We are a society obsessed with the passage of time. We divide the movements of the sun and moon into neat intervals that have questionable accuracy when calculating the incremental movements of these heavenly bodies. To aid our conceived passage of time, we often place imaginary boundaries to cement us to the invention of time. Traveling through the world, time is interpreted according to the convenience and understanding of the individual and culture.

Universally, we look to the sun, moon, and stars to alert us to daily or yearly events and functions. Each geographic location gauges the sun's and moon's energy and uses that knowledge to plant or harvest, plan events, and gauge weather formations. For many years, patterns were observed and formulas created; the result created the vital tools of everyday life-calendars and almanacs. We tend to be active during the day when the sun is full; as it wanes we turn our attention to quiet endeavors and ultimately sleep.

Even though we are looking at the same sun and moon, different cultures seem to interpret the celestial movements differently as to when the day begins and ends.

Taking the cue from the Old Testament, the State of Israel as well as many observant Jews honor the beginning and end of the day at sunset. Taking their interpretation from Genesis: "God separated the light from the darkness. The light was called Day, and the darkness called Night. And there was evening and there was morning, the first day."

The observance of Sabbath each Friday Night and Saturday Day begins Friday at sundown. This observation varies greatly the farther you live from the equator. In the summer in the northern hemisphere, the days are long; sunset could be 9 p.m. Conversely, in the winter the sunset would be early, even as early as 4 p.m. Careful attention must be given to the exact time each day begins, which continually fluctuates.

When teaching in Israel, I found it very confusing to start the day when the appearance of darkness tells me the day ends. On my teaching schedule, which usually simply states Friday, Saturday, etcetera, it now said Friday Eve and Friday Day. My confusion grew. Is Friday Eve what I understand as Thursday night? With patience and great understanding the staff, to quell my perplexity, reverted to the "western" way of delineating day and night.

Removing all the religious and mental conditioning, the continual and predictable movement of the heavenly bodies seem to at least delineate very clearly what is night and what is day.

In India, the daily ritual bathing and prayer is relegated to sunrise. Due to the simplicity and lack of electricity in the rural villages, they are often devoid of clocks or other means of telling time. The job of master timekeeper is relegated to the predictability of the sun. As the dawn lightens the night, they awake and with the rising sun the day is born to the sound of prayers and chanting. A good morning it is!

For some curious reason, in the west we start our day at the darkest time of the night. Seems to me it must have been a compromising committee decision. Sitting in a windowless room, one committee member might have said, "Let's start the day at dawn, when the sun rises." "No better to start at sunset." "Okay let's compromise—we start the day at midnight!"

Each year we spend countless amounts of money on

the purchase of timepieces. The costs vary from a couple of dollars to many thousands. Some are gold, others whimsical. The new models tell us time and much, much more. They can remind us of an appointment or a task to be done. Yet, with all this, we still tend to be late, causing tension and stress.

We have a unique expectancy that fuels our stress, causing resentment and strife among friends and colleagues alike—it is called *waiting*. The need to *wait* is an interesting concept. *Waiting* for someone who is late, we become impatient, irritable and even angry. If we expect someone to be at a certain place at a prescribed time, when they are not there, we *wait*. Some people, though, are habitually late and we come to expect that, even altering our own time schedule to reflect the lateness.

A tribal man in his native village was quizzed about this phenomenon. He was emphatic that they neither have the word *or* the concept, *wait*. Not sure he understood what was being asked, the interviewer reviewed.

"How do you tell someone you will be somewhere, without a timepiece?"

"I look to the sun and we agree when the sun is in this position two more times we will meet at the mountain."

"Hmmm, okay. So what happens if you get there at the prescribed time and she is not there?"

"I am there."

"Then you are waiting."

"Not waiting, I am there."

"What do you do until she comes?"

"Whatever I need to do or do nothing."

"Do you get irritated if the sun is in its third position in the sky and she is still not there?"

"Why should I become irritated? I am there."

The exasperated investigator realized that he was unable to convey the concept of "waiting" to the native. He concluded that time is relevant to each culture and the notion of "waiting" was a perception based on one's experience. Best to relax if we happen to arrive in advance of our potential appointment, rather than the tension-filled *waiting*.

*Namaste, When I am in the place of love and oneness,
I understand everything, Namaste.*

Infinite Like the Sky

The *Vishudda Chakra* vibrates as the color blue, like the sky. Since its element is ether, the symbology encompasses not only the color but our expansion into the infinite. The hue is comforting and allows for an experience free of boundaries and limitations.

This color is often portrayed in religious art depicting the heavens, often housing puffy white clouds. Surrounding Mother Mary, we often find this celestial color reflected in her garb. It's a frequent enough occurrence that there is a color called Divine Mother Blue.

In Asian art, we find deities painted with blue skin, encouraging the observer to look beyond the boundaries of the physical restrictions, rather allowing the celestial color to lead us to the concept of infinity through spirituality.

The vastness of understanding that is conveyed in this chakra has its roots in the concept of being boundless and infinite. The term *understanding* conjures up the image of trying to think how something is done, made, or conceived. This is not the same type of understanding present in this chakra. The description of *Vishudda*, meaning purity, combines with the infinite to give us an understanding that is beyond what the cognitive mind is able to comprehend.

Exhausting our narrow understanding, we are propelled into an infinite understanding that expands the perimeters of the mind beyond all limitations. We are then able to invent, compose, appreciate, and accept that which surpasses the ordinary mind. Many of the great inventions and scientific discoveries had to reach deep into the infinite to give us the knowledge which enhances our lives daily.

Hearing, Listening, and Speaking

Within the etheric realm comes the ability to hear sounds and understand the meaning behind them. The subtlest of the senses, hearing allows us to commune with the outside world.

This sense is unique, as it is the first sense to come and the last to go. In the womb, floating in our own special world, we are in the constant presence of sound. Some exaggerated sounds emanate from our mother's body, digestive sounds and the ever-present heart, keeping its rhythmical beat of life.

The famous Music Museum in Vienna hosts a special room. Dimly lit, one is greeted by an otherworldly feeling. Directly in the center of the room is a large round pulsating object, emitting the sound of a heartbeat, a mother's heartbeat, as heard by the fetus in the womb. Staying present, we are able to transcend the mind's doubts and be transported to a simpler time when it was just us and the sound.

My dear friend, about to deliver her fifth child, entrusted me with her precious daughters while she availed herself of a professional team at the hospital. She summoned me one morning as the telltale signs of labor approached. I arrived in time to wish her well and enjoy the company of the four sweet angels. Off she went to deliver the long-awaited boy, adding a male representative to the brood.

To ease any anxiety about Mom in the hospital, we began to rehearse what would happen when we got the call to meet their new brother.

"When we arrive at the hospital we will all hold hands and walk together. We have to be very quiet, as people are ill and resting. Do you understand?" Four little heads bobbed a *yes*.

"We will then find the room Momma is in and we'll meet your new brother. Won't that be fun?" An exuberant chorus of cheers resounded.

Again I repeated the drill, hoping that all would go as planned.

When the long-anticipated call arrived, we were rehearsed and ready to welcome their new brother. As practiced, the girls piled into the car and, with overflowing enthusiasm, we drove to the hospital. The gentle reminder of quiet and handholding lasted only until we entered the lobby.

From what seemed like a distant universe, we heard ear-shattering screams. As if given a signal, the girls abandoned my hands and took off like sprint runners determined to win the race. Attempting to shush them and keep up at the same time, I finally gave up as they entered the newborn's room. The squealing we heard on arrival was now targeted to this very spot.

As soon as the girls laid eyes on their new brother, after months of anticipation, in unison, they jumped up on the bed. Four squealing voices reassured him that all his sisters were present. The crying instantaneously ceased—total silence from the newborn—*he was home.*

As onlookers, we were at first stunned by the scene before our eyes. On careful review, we recalled that during the pregnancy the girls' great anticipation of his arrival led them to drum, talk, and sing to their brother in utero. He got to know them by their dulcet tones. When his journey through the birth canal was complete, he arrived to the sounds of strangers. Where are my sisters? I don't hear them at all. Unable to express it in words, his cries summoned them.

If we are able to hear sounds in the womb, what happens when we go in the opposite direction? Many are correlating birth and death, observing many similarities. Life is at the beginning of the cycle and death at the other end, or are they? Rather than thinking of life and death as linear, if we take the two ends and join them, a circle is formed. We then understand that life is a continuum rather than an end. The sense of hearing is present through the whole cycle.

We have heard many tales of people in comas, under anesthesia, with serious conditions, even near death, who have reported hearing sounds, voices, and prayers. Reading uplifting poems, prayers, and stories to someone in the last stages of life can aid their transition. In some cases it could even convince them to stay a bit longer here on earth.

These insights and revelations come from our own observation, the religious community, and sometimes stems from the medical profession.

Dr. Frank spent many hours a day sitting quietly at the head of his patients, watching gauges. It was often tedious, and boredom did creep in from time to time, but that was all just part of his job as an anesthesiologist. His mind would often wander to the patient's wellbeing, wondering where their consciousness resided at the moment when they were lying unconscious on the operating table. His wondering led him to experiment by talking to the patient's unconscious, even as their bodies and minds were unable to respond. He spoke the phrases silently, thinking that nobody else could hear, but it seems someone did hear.

"They are going to cut now, begin to withdraw the blood from the incisional area."

"Everything looks really good; your doctor did a great job of getting it all."

"The site is being sewed up, bring in some white cells to ward off infection."

"When you return to your room, when you awaken, you will feel only minimal discomfort. You will then heal very quickly."

He began to use a similar affirmation with each patient, varying it according to the person and procedure. It became part of his daily routine. After some time, his practice started to grow exponentially; he became curious, having done this work for twenty-plus years, why the sudden growth?

One by one he asked the surgeons who normally did not refer to him, why they had changed. "We have heard that when *you* administer the anesthesia the patients seem to do better. Less bleeding was noted as well as lower incidence of infection, and the patients leave the hospital sooner. We do not know what you do differently than the other anesthesiologists, but whatever it is it seems to benefit the patients. You have our business!"

With an inward smile, he tried to understand what was actually happening in his "conversations" with the patients. His rational mind could not comprehend it but going beyond, he began to relate to a whole new dimension to the sense of hearing. The ability to hear that which the ordinary hearing cannot experience is easily "heard" through the extraordinary sense of *clairaudience*.

Hear or Speak

The sense of hearing is complemented by the desire to speak. Hearing is a passive sense, speech is active. It is said we have two ears but only one mouth, so it is best to listen twice as much as we speak. A good motto for most of us to live by.

Often the ability to listen is upstaged by the ability to speak. They are really two parts of the whole. According to Yoga teachings there are three aspects to all the senses. The object of sense would then be transmitted through the ether to the organ of sense, which in this case would be the ears. From the ears, the sound goes to the brain which interprets the sound.

A sound may be produced from across the room. The sound wave then travels through the ether to be received by the outer ear, which then swirls it around, depositing the vibration in the inner ear. From there it is processed by the brain so we can identify the sweet sounds. For speech, the process goes in the opposite direction. The brain decides what it wants to say, the vocal cords produce the sound, it is projected through the mouth and tongue and thrust into the ether where it is received by someone's ear and hopefully heard and understood. Both of these are part of the normal functioning of the *Vishudda Chakra*. When unencumbered by the mind's chatter, we are able to hear, listen, and speak with purity.

Many of us may be squandering this precious gift by exposing the delicate ears to loud sounds on a regular basis. The need to yell over loud music can give an easy hint that the decibels are too high. With the advent of ear phones or buds, we are doing a disservice to our ability to hear. The outer ear is specifically designed to spiral the sound until it finally slides into the ear canal. This allows the harshness of sound to be tempered and softened so as to not offend the delicate structure. When that is bypassed by placing the buds directly in the ear, the loud sounds go rushing directly into the canal and into the inner ear. After some time, the ability to hear is shrouded. This has become such a growing issue that the average forty-year-old of today has the hearing the average sixty-year-old had twenty-five years ago! Maybe we need to rethink the way we listen to music.

The human body has a way of adapting to circumstances in mysterious ways. When we think of sound, most of us think of hearing with the ears. But what if we could hear other ways? There is a large community of people who, for a variety of reasons, are unable to hear exterior sounds. Yet, they maintain a very active communication by enticing their creative minds to find other pathways. The whole system of sign language allows communication when the sense of hearing is not giving the necessary results.

For those who have been born without the ability to hear or the loss occurred at an early age, other ways to "hear" are explored. Since sound is vibration, why not implore the whole body to get involved with listening. It may not be possible to distinguish words or a particular sound, but the vibration can be felt. That is how we can witness those with hearing impairment or even total loss, swaying to the rhythms on the dance floor.

Some years back, during a silent retreat, as was the custom, I offered mantra initiation on behalf of my teacher, Swami Satchidanandaji. A mantra is a sound syllable extracted from an ancient language, where the power is enshrined in the vibration rather than the meaning. With constant repetition, the mind becomes calm and steady. A one-pointedness arises, allowing consciousness to transcend the thinking mind and settle in a place of stillness and peace. It is a very respected technique that crosses all religious traditions.

The initiation begins by introducing a sacred mantra and having the initiate repeat it until assurance is reached that the pronunciation is correct. A gentle touch, usually on the top of the head, imparts energy from the master to student. Sri Swamiji used to liken it to putting a few drops of live culture from an established source into some nicely warmed milk. After a time, the parent culture takes hold and the new culture has now made the milk into yogurt. This newly minted yogurt is then able to pass its culture on to another.

One particular initiation created challenges. On reviewing the applications, it appeared that one of the initiates was visually impaired and one was hearing impaired. I did not think there needed to be much adjusting for the visually impaired student, as she was able to hear and repeat. I would just need to verbally spell the foreign words for her.

But what to do with the hearing impaired student? I had learned that to "hear" music, a balloon could be requisitioned and held near the speaker. This allowed the vibration from the music to resonate through the ether into the balloon and ultimately into the body. This gave me a pathway for new creativity.

Traditionally, the new initiates wear a particular type of white Indian-style clothes. Coming unprepared, the blind woman did not have the necessary garb. On discovering this, the deaf woman generously offered her extra outfit. Wondering if the size would comply, she brought the outfit over a half an hour before the initiation. Without a sound, the outfit was taken out of the bag and held up against the body of the borrower. However, due to her visual impairment, she was unable to see if it fit. Leaving it to the two of them to come up with a creative solution, they both turned their backs to each other. As the bodies met they, in unison, touched the top of first their own head and then slipped it behind to measure the other's head. Behold it was a perfect fit. We all cheered, both aloud and with mimed clapping!

One challenge out of the way, the next loomed large. How would I manage to communicate the mantra and correct pronunciation to someone unable to hear me? First, I tried to clearly mouth the mantra exaggerating the lip gestures. We both tried, but it was not the right fix. Asking for divine guidance, an idea came. Placing her hand on my throat, I began to repeat the mantra. Looking at the phonetic spelling, feeling the physical vibration from my throat, while observing my lip movements, we set off on our journey to learn the mantra. After a few minutes, her pronunciation still a distance away from its target, I was ready to say close enough. Our cheering section comprised of the other initiates met her tenacity and rallied me to continue.

After a time, my mind began to wander and was abruptly summoned back to the moment by the most beautiful sound. Our dear tenacious soul, seeking to know the truth, was repeating the mantra perfectly, with as much gusto as I have ever experienced. Withdrawing her hand from my neck, she continued to recite the sacred sound. Other than the repetition, the only other sounds in the room were the sobs that matched the cascading of tears on all our faces. A victory for the transmission of sacred sounds.

Namaste, When I am in the place of love and oneness, I understand everything, Namaste.

Clairaudience, Clear Hearing

The ability to hear, being a very precious gift, comes with the ability to transcend ordinary hearing as the *Vishudda* awakens and begins to vibrate on a higher frequency. When we first begin our exploration of chakras, we often relay their attributes as if they are physical manifestations. We are able to relate to the colors and the senses as we experience and perceive them. When we move to the next level, the perception of physicality fades. We are now exposed to a deeper level of sense perception.

In the *Anahatha Chakra,* we learned of *clairsentience*, the ability to *feel* that which is not felt by the physical touch. With the *Vishudda,* we are graced with *clairaudience*, the ability to *hear* that which cannot be heard with the physical ears.

We often "hear" a warning that others do not or hear the phone ring moments before the actual sound, as well as other "otherworldly" occurrences. These extraordinary events cause an uneasiness for many who choose to rationalize them away or have them quickly forgotten. Yet, they are as much a part of us as the physical hearing. The subtle tend to be shyer and easily taunted by our doubts, causing them to retreat. If we are able to welcome this gift and honor its use, it will strengthen and be a constant companion, opening us to worlds only imagined.

There are many accounts of people about to board an airplane who are cautioned by that ethereal voice to make other arrangements; those heeding the message are often rewarded by news of delays or worse. "Don't take the freeway," my friend was cautioned. "That is ridiculous it is so much quicker," the rational mind retorted. When stalled for more than an hour in traffic, she wondered why she had not listened to the quiet message.

The messaging can be of the type mentioned above, or a connection can occur that could only take place beyond our normal understanding.

Bypassing the Mind

At an international Yoga conference in Switzerland, I was invited to a private *Satsang* (the company of others who share the same truth) with a very well respected *Yogiraj* (great Yogi). His path was one of asceticism and austerity. His appearance reflected the truth of his path, with matted locks dripping on the floor, wooden shoes, and the nails of both toes and fingers inches long. In the company of this great being, donned in my silk monks' robes I felt a bit self-conscious and *very* worldly. Despite the outer coverings and the divergence of our paths, I knew that our hearts held the same truth.

A vow of silence, entered into many years before, led him to comfortably converse with students by placing a word or two on a chalkboard. The writing was coded in his native language, unfamiliar to those of us attending the *Satsang*. One of his senior disciples, proficient in the swami's teachings and mother tongue, would then expound upon it. Swami Sri la Sri would nod "yes" or "no" at varying speeds, according to the level of accuracy.

After some time my mind, fascinated by our apparent differences, began to wander to the diverse way we presented the essential teachings of Yoga. I had studied Yoga for many years through an abundance of great teachers (mostly Indian), which I then filtered and reorganized through my western cultural understanding. Swami Sri la Sri, being born and raised in India, had a more traditional Vedic view of the same teachings. Yet, we both lived and taught Yoga from our hearts. Suddenly, I was reeled back to the *Satsang* by Swami Sri la Sri's gaze, gesturing to *me* to answer a question.

My dazed expression prompted his disciple to restate the question in English. I remained silent as I struggled to understand what was expected of me. Swami Sri la Sri accelerated his writing on the board, attempting to explain a complex concept simply. His disciple was struggling to clarify (with the impatient prompting from his teacher) what the *heart* of this teaching was expressing. Again, Swami Sri la Sri turned around and waved at me, hoping I could shed some light on this important teaching.

Consciously, I leapt into the depth of my limited understanding, not finding the ability needed to be of service. Suddenly a place previously unknown to me opened, as I was propelled into a vastness beyond my conscious mental patterning. I began to speak, observing that I was *actually interpreting* what he was thinking *and* in a foreign tongue. The words on the chalkboard made no sense to my mind; yet, I seemed to be getting a direct transmission, propelled by a deep resonance with the Swami. Could it be we were both visiting the same place of deep understanding, merging with the infinite?

His rapid head-bobbing indicated that the translation was correct, so I continued. After some minutes, the stream of transmission slowed down. I felt otherworldly; something wonderful had taken place. Again, this time with less prompting, I continued to interpret his words. "To look at both of us one would think we were very different, but clothes and styles neither form truth nor detract from it. She (meaning me) has her way of expressing the great teachings of Yoga for westerners, as I to the traditional Indians. The essence of the teachings is one and the same. When hearts speak with integrity *that* is Yoga." Hearing myself say that, I was embarrassed, anticipating 'my' thoughts had returned. But, looking over at Swami Sri la Sri, his eyes were beaming as his long locks swayed in an endorsement.

"[The Human] mind stretched to a new idea never goes back to its original dimensions."
—Oliver Wendell Holmes.

Namaste, When I am in the place of love and oneness, I understand everything, Namaste.

We can understand through these examples that the rational mind is hard-pressed to make sense of this extrasensory perception—*clairaudience*. Also encased in this phenomenon is the rarified ability to express words or sentiments that often prove to be profound truths. Wondering where the knowledge comes from, we have only to look to this chakra of purity to find the answer. Hearing of great women and men forging innovative discoveries, many proclaim that plants, animals, and humans—both living and dead—communicated with them. Causing a great deal of skepticism among the "rational" it is nonetheless an accurate and often beneficial exchange.

This knowledge, whether developed from birth or later, be it cultivated or spontaneous, becomes the beacon for some people's life's work. We have heard of geniuses graced with the ability to compose music from a very early age—great musicians like Joshua Bell, who at age four started playing the violin after he was discovered stretching rubber bands across the dresser knobs and plucking them in tune with his mother's piano music.

Mozart, whose music has been proved to stimulate intelligence in babies while still in utero (his was some of the music often played through headphones on a pregnant belly), was composing symphonies at age six when most us were still just learning how to spell and add.

These extraordinary talents are not limited to the music world; we can admire them in all milieus. Looking to zoos and animal parks, some young trainers seem to have a special affinity to speak and listen to the animals, allowing them to be understood and respected.

This *clairaudience* also reverberates through the plant world. The idea of communing with a plant seems quite ominous to many of us. At least with humans and animals, there seems to be some favorable interaction when conversing (although I have heard numerous complaints from parents claiming their children do not hear them, meaning that the offspring do not care to listen)! Pets also have selective hearing when told to stay off the couch or not to beg at the table.

Communing with plants seems to be yet a step further from our human interaction skills. Admittedly, I have sung and talked to my plants and they did respond by staying alive for many years! A special gift is fostered in some who commune with healing plants and herbs. How do they know that one plant will help medicinally and another will harm? Do plants actually speak, revealing their healing properties?

The Native Americans were very much convinced of this and listened closely. The whisper from the plants was the key to unlocking the secrets of the medicinal properties, ready to soothe and comfort. The way to achieve this union with plants is through connection, love, compassion, and respect. It is the Namaste moment, of realizing that we, the earth, and her plants are one.

While living in Los Angeles, I was visiting a holy garden which housed some of the original cactus that had been nurtured and tended by Luther Burbank, an American botanist, horticulturalist, and a pioneer in agricultural science.

While he developed more than 800 strains and varieties of plants over his 55-year career, the one he is most well-known for is the spineless cactus. The spines on the prickly pear (and other cacti) are there for protection. The sharp spines are fitted with the capacity to detach easily when touched, a very effective defense against being eaten.

Being a deeply spiritual man, he began to dialogue with

the spiny cactus. Assuring it he would be its protector, he coaxed the plant to grow without spines. I saw the astonishing results of this pact—a large, lustrous, and spineless prickly pear cactus! Reverently, as it reflected the sun, I gently caressed its soft surface. It had grown in trust for many years and was now over ten feet tall. As I was reveling in its beauty I noticed tiny spines beginning to form at the base. Curious, I studied the great monolith closer when tears spontaneously stung my eyes. Some foolhardy youths, wanting to be remembered in perpetuity, had carved their names into her beautiful body, ignoring the fact that plants are a living part of the earth, as are we. From that point of violence, the cactus remembered its protective defenses and summoned the spines to flourish.

Faith, Prayer, and Higher Communication

The *Vishudda Chakra* brings the concept of Faith, Prayer, and Higher Communication into clear light. To fully appreciate a concept, situation, or person, we must transcend our limits to embrace the larger understanding beyond our worldly experiences. The leap into the world of faith allows us to experience truth with ourselves. Faith does not need to be in something or someone outside of ourselves; it can reverberate with our own higher consciousness. We learn at a very early age that communication can be with someone who no one else experiences.

Developing the ability to speak to the Divine, in *any form we choose*, often comes when we have exhausted the normal channels of communication. What we call prayer is simply a way to prompt our version of a higher power to be partners in our myriad of endeavors.

Prayers can be directed to the Divine within or to an outward presence. Much of the time, we go back and forth according to the moment and mood. Most of the summoning manifests the greatest power of prayer in difficult times. When all other avenues have been exhausted and the enormity of the situation becomes too great to bear alone, we then pray to someone else out there as a separate entity or manifestation to help us cope. We are really just summoning all the positive energy and celestial beings that are standing by to make our lives easier in all ways. Extending and reaching our arms toward the sky, we surrender in prayer.

Early in my spiritual practice, I learned to dedicate the fruits of my practices to something or someone in need. This kept me steady in spiritual pursuits, knowing it was not only for me. Under the altar would be a small book that held the names of those recipients in need of prayers. This was the start of my wonderment about faith and prayer.

Often, we pray as if it is a bargaining chip. We make promises (as if the Divine needs our bargains) that are often discarded when the desired effect is wrought. Out of courtesy, we say thank you and express gratitude, even to a stranger, when our request is granted. Is divine intervention any less worthy of a thank you? We search for clues to assess the fulfillment of the prayer and gauge our gratitude accordingly. Looking into how prayer affects not only the receiver but also the transmitter keeps us in the rhythm of prayer and higher communication.

Prayer itself is a state of action, something we ask for by request or petition, for ourselves or others. The intention is to reach into the depth of our being or receive celestial guidance to formulate an antidote to a situation clearly out of our control. To do this effectively, our minds and hearts seek purity. Any hint of personal desire or prejudice will hinder the process. That is why the *Vishudda* reigns over that aspect of prayer.

When the prayer request has been completed, the results have been transmitted through the ether or *prana*, we await reception. Calling on the ability to transcend the awareness of time, we hold no expectation; our request has been sent. It is a fruitless venture to try to assess if our prayers are effective. With our limited understanding, often it is not possible to know what effect was needed and if it was actualized. The best way to affect someone's health or situation is to pray with abandonment, honoring the person's destiny and life's purpose without interference or preferences from us. This vital aspect to prayer is often overlooked.

The offering of gratitude is essential, whether the results of the prayer are to our liking or not. A simple whisper of "thank you" seals the gratitude in our hearts and catapults it into the universe, encouraging a revisit on our next request.

"More things are wrought by prayer than this world dreams of." —Alfred, Lord Tennyson

Namaste, When I am in the place of love and oneness, I understand everything, Namaste.

Long Distance Prayer

For millennia, custom called people of like hearts and minds together to pray, most often for loved ones known to them. Proven effective, this continues today. Often in churches, temples, and many varied places of worship there will be a time in the service where congregants will speak the name of those in need. The power of group prayer is legendary.

In the 21st century, anecdotal information is no longer the norm. Everything needs to be proven and documented. Knowing the importance of prayer and the necessity to prove its efficacy, a group of medical professionals designed a protocol to study long distance prayer.

They decided that anonymity was paramount if the results were to coincide with the hypothesis that prayer, when impersonal, was as or even more effective as knowing the recipient personally. They proposed that devoid of personal attachment and desperation, the power increased.

They recruited a group of patients afflicted with AIDS and distributed the names to religious institutes of varied denominations and geographic locations. The study also included a control group that was told they were being prayed for but, in actuality, none of their names were given. No screening was implemented for prejudices, although the researchers were well aware that preconceptions often muddy the prayer's intention. The biases stemmed from misinformation about a group of strangers, based on the opposition to their religious values.

Being good religious followers they, nonetheless, accepted their assignment to pray. Each person in the prayer group was given a first name and diagnosis. Nothing more. They were asked to pray at a specific time each day, with any prayer of their choice. It could be traditional wording or something they extracted from their hearts. The important part was to be regular and to direct the energy to the name they were dispensed.

The recipients of these prayers, as well as the control group, were asked to write in their journal as to any changes in their physical or emotional well being. Did they experience reduced pain, fatigue, depression, fear? When the tallies arrived for data collection, science embraced religion. The power of prayer was confirmed by the statements of the patients who were prayed for. All felt tangible improvement in their physical and emotional states since the long-distance prayer began. The control group had no significant effects.

The people who did the praying also had a boost in their physical and mental health, knowing that they had contributed to the well being of others doing what their faith led them to do. When love is shared, even with total strangers, our faith grows and our capacity to understand all, flourishes.

It is preferable to cultivate faith and devotion *before* we are in desperate need. Wholehearted devotion connects us through faith to our source. Learning to trust the power within, we courageously let go and live each moment to the fullest. That, after all, is how life is doled out to us, one moment at a time.

A young woman was enjoying her daily task of picking berries in a nearby woodland. She was slowly inspecting each fruit before picking it. Hearing a rustle close by, she spotted a very wild and hungry looking tiger. Throwing her bucket aside, she ran like the wind. Stopping short, she found herself on the precipice of a deep and rugged canyon. The tiger so close she could hear it breathing, she spotted an overhanging branch of a large tree. With great courage and no other choice, she leaped off the cliff and narrowly caught the branch. Hanging over the ravine, she felt a moment of safety. The branch, creaking under her weight, began to snap. She knew that it often took a branch three snaps to break and with that she would be plunged to her demise.

She had never been a woman of faith, but it seemed like it might be a good time to start. With the tiger just feet away, she could almost hear him repeating a meal prayer with *her* as the main course.

With great hesitation, she looked up at the heavens, just as the second snap of the branch was heard. "Is there anyone up there?" She waited, not really expecting a response.

"Yes, my child I am here."

"Really, there is someone there! All these years I doubted, never prayed or went to a service. But that is great, please get me out of this situation."

"Do you have faith?"

"Yes, of course, I have faith." We promise and claim anything at a time of great peril, especially when asking for help.

"Okay, if you have total faith, then LET GO!"

Panic set in. She looked at the hungry tiger. She eyed the branch connected now by only by a single fiber hovering over the abyss.

Looking up once again she yelled, "IS THERE ANYBODY *ELSE* UP THERE?!!!!"

Namaste, When I am in the place of love and oneness,
I understand everything, Namaste.

Meditation on the Vishudda Chakra

• • • • •

Allow the body and mind to become quiet.

Feel yourself softening into a deep stillness and peace.

Close the eyes.

Take in a few deep breaths and let them out very slowly.

Bring the awareness to the Throat Center.

There, awaiting your awareness, is a whirling vortex of energy emanating a glowing vibration of blue color reminiscent of the infinite sky.

This vibration generates outward as the *Vishudda Chakra*. It connects us to the force of purity, understanding and faith, and our use of it.

Observe your breath as it flows in and out with ease. (one minute)

Listen to the swishing sound it makes when it enters the body in the inhalation—*soooo*.

Hear the sound as it leaves the body on the exhalation—*hum*.

Be still and listen to the sounds of the vital life force entering and leaving your being.

Inhale *Soooo*, Exhale *hum*. Inhale *Soooo*, Exhale *hum*. Inhale *Soooo*, Exhale *hum*.

Continue until the sound is well established. (one minute)

Inhale, *soooo,* and with the next exhale begin to softly repeat *hum* aloud. The mantra *hum* can be said as a word, or create a humming sound within and repeat that.

Continue to hear *soooo* on the inhalation and audibly repeat *hum* on the exhalation.

With each repetition, imagine yourself standing on the earth, gazing at the infinite blue sky.

Hear the humming sound vibrating through the air and ether, infusing *prana* through your body, mind, and senses.

Imagine it gracing us with the ability to understand even that which is beyond understanding. (a few moments)

Feel your entire being illuminated with faith in both the known and unknown.

Continue to repeat *hum* as the prana merges with the pulsating universe. (one minute)

The universal energy pulsates through your body, enlivening each cell.

The thoughts begin to vibrate with the rhythm.

The emotions let go and dance to the beat.

Feel this serene energy attracting clarity.

Use this moment to shine that clarity on a particular situation that may be impacting your life.

Focus the sound vibration on this issue.

Allow the mantra *hum*, to shine a beacon of clarity, resolving any misunderstanding.
(one minute)

Begin to focus on the blue color of the *Vishudda Chakra*. Observe its vastness and notice as luminosity radiates both inward and outward.

Appreciate our developed sense of hearing, through the sounds of nature, beautiful music, precious words and voices.

Allow the verbal repetition of *hum* to quiet as you draw inward.

Listen to the mantra as it is silently repeated deep within.

The singular sound once repeated aloud merges with the sound of the universe, called as *Pranava*.

Be still and listen as the universal sound, the *Pranava*, reverberates.

Allow the sound to become the vibration that continues to reverberate into infinity. (one minute)

As *soooo hum* continues, notice how the body is enriched by the vibration.

The mind and emotions calm when infused with the cosmic vibration.

Feel the radiance of blue sky, the color of

understanding and purity, infusing your entire being. (a few moments)

Bring the awareness back to the throat center at the *Vishudda Chakra*.

Slowly and very gently bring the awareness back to the breath.

Notice how still and calm it has become.

Slowly begin to deepen the breath.

Feel the awareness return to the body, mind, and emotions.

Continue to sit quietly for a few minutes as the scope of the universal sound, *Pranava*, transmitted from the *Vishudda Chakra*, radiates outward.

Create an affirmation allowing *soooo hum* to continually vibrate in tune with the universe.

Connecting to the sound of the universe, we experience oneness.

● ● ● ● ●

Namaste, When I am in the place of love and oneness, I understand everything, Namaste.

Chapter Six

Ajna Chakra

When I am in a place of love and oneness

I know everything

Wisdom and Knowledge

Overnight Train to Moscow

At a conference center in northern Finland, we gathered for a briefing on what to expect traveling into what was, at that time, communist Russia. We were a group of healers and clergy from across the United States, about to venture into still-forbidden territory to meet our counterparts who worked for the good of Russia. The excitement and expectation was peaking, as we would go back to Helsinki to board an overnight train taking us deep into Mother Russia and on to Moscow City.

While there was great enthusiasm among the travelers, we could not ignore all the years of fear and indoctrination we had received about Russia. Some of us remember hiding under our school desks for fear that "The Russian were coming to get us." Since the imaginary invasion never happened, our trepidation was temporarily assuaged. Could all of the stories we have been told be true? If even a portion was real, what then? We were about to find out. Tucking fear in our knapsacks, we went forward with unbridled fervor.

Spending a few days at the retreat center had been to share hopes and relate concerns of what we had heard *and* what it could be like. Many of the families of those present injected anxiety along with pleas to cancel trip plans, fearful of their loved ones going into the unknown, especially communist Russia.

We were also prepared for what we could encounter going through border control and customs. Each country has its restrictions as to what is permitted to pass through its borders. Some countries search for drugs, others firearms and explosives. For Russia, religious and political articles were forbidden. We were all asked to bring small trinkets for hostess gifts and were told specifically not to bring anything that might be construed as religious or political propaganda.

One kind man had used his own money to print up 1500 plastic coated buttons, some with the word *Mir (peace)* and others with *I Love You*, in both English and Russian. He envisioned the buttons broadcasting the messages of love and friendship. Asking each of us to take a bag of the buttons to place in our suitcases and carry-ons, he was concerned the messages could be misconstrued as political or spiritual propaganda. Disbursing them among many travelers would assure that no one person would have the lion's share, and the smaller quantities would, hopefully, fall within the hosting country's stringent rules.

I was not in any way interested in carrying the buttons, which I perceived as silly and gauche. And I certainly had no intention of wearing one. I was much too dignified and sophisticated to do that!

As life would have it, the "button man" was my next door neighbor at the hotel. As I strategically tried to sneak past his room on the way to breakfast the day of departure, he magically appeared with bags filled with buttons. "Please help carry these beyond the borders," he pleaded. My heart opened where my head balked. I reluctantly took the bag, went back to my room and stashed it in the very bottom of my carry-on bag.

Finally, it was time to go on our adventure, and as I slung my knapsack over my shoulder the contraband buttons faded to only a memory. We were on our way to board the train at the Helsinki station. Informed that the train would stop at the Finnish-Russian border for an engine swap, we snuggled into our shared compartments for some rest in preparation for our very full itinerary. The Finnish engine needed to be exchanged for a Russian engine so that we could continue our journey. It seems the tracks varied in their placement from one country to another.

It was in the dead of night when our train ground to a stop at the border. Russian soldiers boarded each car; our passports and visas were scrutinized, our bags meticulously inspected. I peered out the window for a glimpse of the people I had been taught to fear since childhood. Who were these evil people who scare little innocent children? I was now getting my first look. They did look ominous in their uniforms, with their machine guns and big German Shepherd dogs. I noticed my heart beating faster and my palms sweating as the leaden footsteps quickened.

The moment of truth came as the door to my cabin swung open, and the enemy and I were face to face. *Except*, he did not look like an enemy; he looked like a sweet young man with deep blue eyes. It caused me to remember that saying from the Revolutionary War, "Don't shoot 'til you see the whites of their eyes." I now understood why the saying was so notable. When you are so close that you can look into someone's eyes, seeing them as the enemy is more difficult. They then become a person with thoughts, hopes, and fears—just like you.

The soldier came in and, after examining my passport and visa, started going through my luggage. I was still a bit flustered by the appearance of the *enemy*, and I paid little attention to what he was doing. Then I remembered the buttons. What would happen when he found them? After all, they were not my idea to start with, I rationalized. I was silently working myself up into quite an unpleasant state.

Meanwhile, he was rummaging through the knapsack, his head halfway in. Then I heard three little words that made my heart explode with joy and changed my entire life. "I love you," he said in clear English.

I couldn't believe what I was hearing, but there in the star-filled night of communist Russia, my enemy was telling me, "I love you." My heart opened so wide the words flew out, "I love you, too." With my pronouncement, he raised his head up and, for a moment in time, the barriers between us melted. We were eye to eye, heart to heart, soul to soul.

With the completion of his duties, he left my cabin. Immediately, I went into my knapsack and found two buttons, one that read *Ya tebya lyublyu* (I love you) and the other *Mir* (peace). I pinned one on my sweater and one on my coat. Those buttons became my constant companions; I wore them every day and night during my entire stay in Russia. I wanted everyone to know, even when facing the enemy, if we look deeply into their eyes we know, *we are one.*

"Out beyond ideas of wrongdoing and right doing there is a field. I'll meet you there. When the soul lies down in that grass, the world is too full to talk about." —Rumi

Namaste, When I am in the place of love and oneness, I know everything, Namaste.

The Ajna Chakra

The *Ajna Chakra*, also known as the third eye, manifests the universal truth of unity, outshining the duality that impacts our everyday consciousness. Holding at its core the basic knowledge that *We are One* with everything, this chakra personifies the term *Namaste* as it transcends the concept of duality. Indeed, we are capable of expressing love in all the chakras, yet in the Ajna, we cannot help but love as the realization of this oneness dawns.

The *Ajna Chakra* grants insight and knowledge undiscernible in our common learning. Rarified, it is no longer beholden to the earth or her elements. It manifests the quality of light as it radiates with a violet color that ascends into ultraviolet.

When our consciousness fully blossoms, *Ajna Chakra* awakens. *Ajna* is derived from the Sanskrit word, *Jnana*, which manifests as wisdom or knowledge. When it surpasses even *Jnana* as we know it, it becomes *Ajna*, beyond wisdom. By placing an A as a prefix we leap a giant step beyond what we are able to learn, to what we experience from this higher level of consciousness. This chakra far surpasses all expectation and propels us beyond the ordinary to a rarified dimension where access is bestowed. Ordinary knowledge, scholars agree, is learned through reading, education, mentoring, and through our life's experiences. *Ajna* propels us beyond the everyday intellectual level, to tap into the cosmic computer.

The great saints, sages, and seekers impart this wisdom gained from deep stages of meditation. When asking to be taught of these great truths, often the response is, "Sit and be still. The wisdom will be revealed to you."

"Please just give me a taste," a student of spiritual

studies may respond.

"I cannot give you knowledge, because it is already within you. Sit and be still."

Often this sublime wisdom is confused with the intellectual knowledge of the *Manipura Chakra*. A certain amount of power and comprehension can be gained from *Manipura*, yet it is worlds apart from the wisdom the universe offers at this center.

One of the key differences is where the knowledge originates. Experiencing knowledge at the *Manipura*, many great ideas and revelations may come. If it is our perception that we are intelligent, and it is coming from us, all the ideas and thoughts stem from the individual mind. Whether the knowledge is random or focused, we mold the concepts into categories to make any hypothesis work. If however, the wisdom originates from the *Ajna Chakra*, the recipient of these truths is often amazed and inspired by the formed concepts. Dwelling even occasionally in the *Ajna Chakra*, we can experience life as a limitless university.

Most people see life as tragedy and comedy, good and bad, pleasurable and painful. When consciousness dwells in the *Ajna Chakra*, those polarities evaporate. Good and bad, pleasure and pain, real and unreal cease to exist. It's all gone! Originating just below the *Ajna Chakra*, the *Ida* and *Pingala Nadis* perpetuate duality as they distribute life-giving *prana* to the five chakras below. As we open to the vastness of this universal knowledge, any prior concepts we've held pale as the wisdom of the *Ajna Chakra* illumines them.

The first ray to leave the opalescent white of the *Sahasara (crown) Chakra* is ultraviolet, unseen by the human eye. It encourages us to see beyond the earth's qualities, revealing only divine qualities. As the cosmic energy continues to manifest, the color becomes discernable to the physical eyes as a pristine violet or purple. It is the highest vibrational color—longest on the color spectrum.

The violet energy is rarified compared to the rest of the hues. Along with radiating a soothing purple, the color seems to convey an inherent spiritual energy as well. Often when meditation focuses at the third eye the transcendental violet hue appears. As the spiritual radiance introduces itself to us, we are lifted to great heights.

For thousands of years, the inspirational color has enchanted many including spiritual beings, royalty, and clergy. It was the luxury of a very few, due to the scarcity of any coloring agent willing to relinquish its sought-after brilliance for dying cloth. Evading the plant world for many years, the only source of this dye was found in rare crustaceans. With the advent of better living through chemistry, we are now able to find vegetable dyes, allowing us to vibrate with this spiritual hue.

Contrary to many people's understanding of the chakras, while the two physical eyes are housed in the proximity of this chakra, the sense of ordinary sight is not. During our adventure with the *Manipura Chakra*, we explored the sense of sight accommodated there. Because of the subtle aspect of this chakra the ordinary senses are not invited, rather the means by which the *Ajna* expresses itself is through *extraordinary* sight, *clairvoyance*. This observation demonstrates that both the subtle nervous system (*nadis*) and chakra system function beyond the confines of the physical reality. As we approach the *Ajna*, this truth becomes more telling.

Being one of only three women invited to speak at a large Yoga conference has not been so unusual in my life as a spiritual teacher. The field, still very much dominated by men, seems by virtue of its subject matter to have a rather high ceiling to break through. Taking it in stride, I choose to speak from the heart, therefore avoiding any temptation toward competitive banter.

This conference was being held at a well-known university, but what made it different was that it was highlighting the wisdom aspect of Raja Yoga, rather than focusing on the physical aspect of Yoga. Raja Yoga, meaning royal yoga, a term used when referring to the wisdom of the Yoga Sutras, immediately set the tone for some high-spirited dialogue.

In preparation for the conference each day, another copy of a perspective from one of the esteemed speakers arrived in my inbox causing my doubts to grow exponentially. Voicing my concerns to the coordinator about the intellectual heights of the papers, he held steadfast in his commitment for me to present at the conference. All of the presenters except for me were college professors. Although I have spent many years of study with great masters from India, the teachings as I present them are as much intuitive as they are practical. Much of what I offer is drawn from my years of personal practice in the Yogic disciplines.

Still holding a large basket of doubts, I agreed to participate. My presentation was to follow a PowerPoint presentation given by a speaker whose only audience seemed to be the sheet of paper he was reading. While listening, I surveyed the group, which was comprised of 90% women.

The second scholar, apparently unaware of this fact, proceeded to instruct this mostly female group on the *correct* posture for meditation. This perfect posture involved tucking the male genitalia under the heel of the foot and applying pressure! Observing the wincing and discomfort from all the female audience, it would prove to be quite the lead-in for my talk! The horrified looks gave me the confidence I needed to present a practical and heart centered assessment of Raja Yoga.

After my well-received talk, I was able to wander into other discourses where I discovered that many, while not talking about male genitalia, were pontificating about the certain aspects of the scripture while ignoring the students or their needs. What surprised me was the lack of personal experience in their teachings, while much of what I was teaching was derived directly from masters or revealed to me in meditation.

On the last evening, our hosts graciously invited everyone for a delicious Indian meal and a *Kirtan* (chanting of the divine name) at a local Yoga Center. The chanting got quite lively and, with the encouragement of the *Kirtan* leader, many of us got up to dance. While whirling, I noticed the group of male scholars looking very uncomfortable, as they were perched on the edge of a bench in the back room where the props for *Asana* (physical postures) were stored.

My encouragement to join the gaiety was met with vigorous head shaking. Not allowing my happiness to be disturbed, I rejoined the inspirational chanting. The next day, unable to understand the events of the previous night, I slipped them into the recesses of my mind and boarded the shuttle to the airport. As fate would have it, I sat next to the professor who had offered the talk before mine the previous day.

Casually chatting (at least I was), my curiosity got in front of me. "I noticed most of the speakers did not participate in the chanting last night. I am curious as to why."

"Oh, I make it a policy never to do spiritual practice."

I was certain my ears were deceiving me. So I asked in another way. The answer remained the same. "But, if you are speaking about spiritual truths wouldn't it be best to have had the experience yourself, instead of the knowledge coming only from books?" I naively asked.

"The opposite," he said. "I do not want my intellectual knowledge to be clouded by my experience of the truths. This way I consider it pure." With what I perceived as a glint in his eye, he then added, "Besides, no one here will remember anything about my talk, except for my comment about the placement of the male genitals!!!"

For one of the few times in my life, I actually was speechless!

"What wisdom can you find greater than Kindness?" —Jean-Jacques Rousseau

Namaste, When I am in the place of love and oneness, I know everything. Namaste.

Three Eyes, Not Two

Our eyes, being our main sensory organ, are constantly giving us feedback and messages from the outer world. About 70% of the information we receive from our senses is from sight. Even as we *hear* a loud sound, automatically we open our eyes to assess if there is any danger or action needed. When touched, we turn around to *see* who it is. We define being awake in the morning as when we open our eyes.

Through the *Manipura Chakra,* the sense of sight is revealed, allowing us to view the world. It is through the two physical eyes that we begin to understand the sense of sight. They prepare us to venture inward, discovering the spiritual sight of the *third eye.* From our experience of "ordinary" seeing, extraordinary sight seems like a marvel.

Devoid of any of the ordinary five senses, the *Ajna Chakra* manifests the rarefied sense of clairvoyance. It allows us the ability to envision other realms and planes of consciousness beyond the physical. This ability is considered by most religious traditions to be mystical and even occult. Usually ascribed to seers, soothsayers, and spiritual beings, it is actually something very attainable for each of us. At first we learn of its existence, and then its function is revealed.

The third eye is acknowledged as the eye of wisdom and discrimination. This extraordinary gift of clairvoyance defines the ability to "see" things that transcend normal vision and gives us insight into future events before they occur.

Passing through the *Vishudda (throat) Chakra,* time ceased to exist. Therefore, ascending to the *Ajna,* we are unencumbered by this great illusion. When we "see" something with this chakra, past, present, future entwine and rather than functioning sequentially it all is happening simultaneously. It might be difficult to perceive whether an event is happening, about to happen, or has happened. Clairvoyance allows past, present, and future to be observed concurrently. When we are released from the constraints of time, events become timeless.

When Thine Eye Becomes Single

As our comfort with the *Ajna Chakra* increases, clairvoyance emerges. Being the primary sensory output for this chakra, the proficiency of the inner "sight" may come spontaneously or be summoned. Regardless of the presence of the third eye, the two physical eyes continue to function for our everyday needs. This duality of sight can easily move back and forth from ordinary to extraordinary perception, as they "see" in different dimensions.

Directing our attention to the inner eye of wisdom, the sensory output allotted to the sense of sight is now directed inward. The subtle energy's desire to move upward through the chakras is accentuated by the physical position the eyes take when they close. Even as we gaze straight ahead, when the eyes gently close they roll upward. If we try to open the eyes of someone who is sleeping or unconscious, this upward rotation will not allow the iris to be seen. Even in our sleep, the subtle energy seeks an upward movement. While awake, it is the sense of sight, propelled by the mind constantly assessing, which keeps us bound to the physical phenomena, preventing us from ascending to lofty heights.

History shows us that many of the advanced civilizations of yore had their roots in the mystical and occult. Today, we seem to be rooted by a set of concrete beliefs that make us apprehensive about venturing far from the logical, scientific, or physical realms that we hold dear.

The pharaohs of ancient Egypt were quite adept in the occult. To this day, we remain fascinated with the culture that perpetuated great advancement in architecture, medicine, and preservation techniques that, with their demise, have retreated back into the occult. From the drawings and the few writings that remain, we understand that many of the methods and advancements instituted were discerned through the wisdom accessed through the third eye.

The decorative headdresses worn by the ancient Egyptians were embellished with an extension, often serpentine, encircling the crown of the head and then wending its way downward to perch on the forehead at the third eye point. Often detailed with highly conductive material like gold and gems, the efficacy was enhanced.

One can only wonder about the caduceus, the medical insignia, which constitutes two entwined serpents twisting around each other in an upward movement. Joined at the base, they remain together until they reach their place of separation just below the third eye. The entwined serpents polarize as the subtle *nadis*, *Ida* and *Pingala,* which rotate around a central axis of unleashed spiritual energy, the *Shushumna*. The two wings above the serpents seem to symbolize the *Ajna Chakra* with its two symmetrical petals representing duality. It seems the Egyptians were gifted with the same wisdom as the Yogis, both cultures recognizing there are two opposing energies formed in the subtle nervous system. The caduceus has become a universally recognized emblem that continues to symbolize balance and healing.

In the Jewish tradition, it is customary among the male orthodoxy to don *tefillin* during prayer. *Tefillin* is a set of small black leather boxes and straps, containing scrolls of parchment inscribed with verses from the Torah. One box is placed on the arm, facing the heart, with the strap winding around the limb, hand and fingers; while the head-*tefillin*, is placed on the forehead at the third eye point. At the most sacred of time of prayer, the *Ajna Chakra* becomes the focus, as it is called upon to see "beyond."

The Muslim tradition seems to directly involve the third eye in daily prayer. Unlike the Egyptians who embellished the third eye with gold and jewels, in Islam the definition of the third eye comes about differently. During prayer recitation, to show humility the body goes into full prostration, the forehead greeting the ground. With continual prayer, a darkened spot on the third eye is generated and becomes an outward symbol of the sacred and devoted ritual.

One of the most recognized and colorful symbols of the third eye is the vermillion red of the Hindu *bindi*. A *bindi* is a red dot that, when placed at the third eye, reminds us who we really are when we are in the place of oneness. It elevates the ability to remember our own divine nature and to see the same in all. It symbolizes the meaning of Namaste. After formal worship or *puja* a small red dot of cum cum, a ritual powder, will highlight the eye of wisdom. As it is seen throughout the day, it reminds the wearer as well as onlookers of their divine nature. The normal preoccupation of assessing the value of clothes or jewelry or social status will instead be directed to the red dot prominently displayed.

Some religious fanatics will go the extreme of piercing or cutting open the forehead in the approximate place where the third eye would be, thinking to create an awakening on the subtle level. Often they reap great disappointment to learn that the physical action has, in this situation, little effect on the subtle.

Within Yoga, the *Ajna Chakra* is an essential chakra for deeper practices. It is considered, along with the *Anahatha (heart) Chakra,* one of two sacred centers of focus for mediation. Encouraging the focus on the inner sight, we transcend the physical world, embracing the light and oneness of our divine essence.

The holy season of Lent in Christianity is initiated by placing holy ash on the forehead in the sign of a cross. As a mystical gesture, it asks us to remember the transcendent meaning of the crucifixion and ascension of Jesus Christ. The placement of the ash has always been curious to me and I have asked many of the observant why the center of the forehead is designated. Not knowing the significance of the third eye to transcend the obvious, the answers are often "it's traditional."

Walking along the *Via Dolorosa,* I experienced a certain level of inward humility. The *Way of Sorrow* is a winding path within the Old City of Jerusalem, believed to be the path that Jesus trod on the way to his crucifixion. I was visiting the holy city that has been honored by Christian, Jews, and Muslims for generations. It is rare to find a place on earth, small yet overflowing with piety and devotion.

Moving at a snail's pace, our small group echoed the immense spiritual resonance of this *camino*. I noticed a large group of pilgrims, led by a rather imposing priest from the Greek Orthodox tradition, walking into a building entered directly from the street. Asking my friends, who had lived in Jerusalem their entire lives, what the building housed, they shrugged their shoulders unknowingly. "Should we follow them and see?" I asked as I turned to enter, my enthusiasm already moving up the staircase. The Orthodox priest continued to lead his flock up the steps, hesitating at the first landing where two prison cells were situated. One had the name lettered on the top, *Barabbas*. Could this be *the* prison that detained Jesus as well as the infamous prisoners, the night before their crucifixion?

Mounting the next set of steps, I began to feel lightheaded. Attributing it to the sublime vibration, I found myself ushered by the Orthodox group into a very small cell. The otherworldly vibration permeated the prison cell that incarcerated Jesus Christ the night before he carried the cross to his death.

Grasping the wall to steady myself, I saw that the dimly lit room revealed holes cut into the wooden harness that restrained his arms and legs entrapping him in this tiny cell. Feeling weakness entering my body, my legs were no longer able to support me. Noticing my state, the priest motioned for me to come to him. As I struggled to right myself, two kind hands took hold of my shoulders, propping me up so I could wend my way over to where he was standing. With a nod of permission from me, the priest took a small soft brush and dipped it into a container of holy oil housed in the prison cell. He then "painted" the sign of the cross on my third eye with the anointed oil. Falling into a swoon, I was escorted to the edge of a small bench. By then my friends had found me and, with one supporting each side, we exited the cell. Arriving back on the *Via Dolorosa,* the air revived me to normal function.

When asked, my friends confessed they had not known of this holy building's existence. "Each time we passed here the door was always bolted shut, we assumed it was just a private home. There was no hint or indication that this doorway concealed the essence of a holy shrine."

This experience was another instance of anointing the *Ajna Chakra*. The knowledge of the third eye continues to be revered through the passage of time, through many different spiritual paths.

> "When the eye becomes single, the whole-body fills with light." —New Testament

The world of science and discovery also honors the wisdom of the third eye. Albert Einstein, a noble scientist, showed humility in making revolutionary discoveries. Being deeply spiritual, he delved into the secrets of the universe, experiencing the awe along with his breakthroughs. When asked how he discovered the properties of light, he was clear to say that he had not discovered it at all. "I meditated on it until it revealed itself to me." It is the clairvoyance held in this chakra that unlocks the mysteries of the ages. Focused mediation allows the essence of all things to be revealed.

Namaste, When I am in the place of love and oneness, I know everything, Namaste.

Our preoccupation with discarding anything that our logical mind cannot comprehend keeps us in intellectual bondage. When we are able to expand our limited vision and beliefs beyond the "proven," we are liberated. Otherwise, we remain tethered to certain known truths, unable to explore the vastness of phenomenal experiences well within our reach. The third eye of wisdom inspires visions, as well as the ability to see illumined beings with clarity. For generations, this subtle manifestation allowed those blessed with these visions to be revered as saints *or* relegated to the demonic realms.

Often it is difficult to prove that it is an actual vision, not just a fantasy the mind conjured up for its amusement. How is it possible to explain or prove something that only *you* can *see*?

There are some cultures and subcultures that accept the ability to see visions as an advancement on their spiritual path. The culture supports and even encourages such visitations. Children are often the recipients of such sightings because their minds are uncluttered, and they have an innocent trust in the etheric. They will recount seeing angels and beings of light appearing to them in times of need or fright. Often, they have accepted these celestial beings as friends to play with at will.

When revealed to skeptical adults, the reactions could be a condescending smile or outright denial. Some bubble-busters try to convince the children that angels do not exist, rather to put away childish ideas and face reality. What a sad thing to say to anyone, especially innocent children. Because the adults were unable to experience the *seeing*, it seems inconceivable that these visions could exist to anyone else.

There are many holy places where the miraculous plays out every day. Believers are welcomed in throngs while the skeptics try to disprove what their physical eyes cannot see and their minds cannot comprehend.

As I've traveled around the world, if a holy shrine is in close proximity, a sojourn is planned. There are three major sites in Europe that have witnessed visitations from

Mother Mary: Lourdes, France; Medjugorje, Bosnia; and Fatima, Portugal. Of these, the most illustrious and well visited is in Lourdes, France. Many are drawn to Lourdes for its spiritual essence and healing waters. The story tells of Saint Bernadette, a humble young girl bearing physical distress, rendering her too ill to keep up with her sisters as they are gathering wood for the family. Books have been written and a movie made about her experience as she waits in a grotto contaminated with germ-infested hospital waste. While waiting for her sisters among the rubble, a vision of a beautiful lady in blue speaks to her. In her innocence, she recounts the vision to the elders, unknowingly provoking rage from the clergy.

They were outraged that she, a simple-minded child, should have a visitation from Mother Mary rather than they, the pious ones. After all, they reasoned, is it not we the clergy that have dedicated our lives to prayer and service to God? If anyone should have a visitation of the Holy Mother, it should be *us*! In their spiritual confusion, they proceeded to discredit Bernadette, trying to commit her to a mental facility.

With her unwavering faith in her vision she eventually convinced the Pope of her relationship with the *beautiful lady enveloped in blue light*. Spirit winning over arrogance, to this day Lourdes draws hundreds of thousands of pilgrims each year to bathe in the healing vibration and waters.

While the details of the story differ, the underlying theme is repeated. When in Bosnia teaching, I was asked if there was any special place I would like to visit. "Medjugorje," was my quick reply. My hosts, being scientific and very practical, hoped I would ask for any other request. No one wanted to escort me. Finally, one sweet woman relented.

It was an arduous trip—trains, buses, cars, hitchhiking—until we finally arrived in the tiny village on the outskirts of the site of the miracle. At the time of my visit, the Virgin Mary was still appearing each evening to the same three children. Before the visitation occurred each evening, all pilgrims and staff, other than the three principal players, were asked to leave. Through photographs and tellings, we were able to observe the children as the wisdom was imparted. Faces aglow, heads tilted slightly back, they were poised to see her form and receive the gifts. Even though we were not permitted to be physically present for the vision, the vibration emitted from the spiritual eminence lay in waiting to elevate the next group of pilgrims.

It is always interesting to note that the visitations are welcomed by the children. Their purity of heart allows the unseen to permeate the cognitive mind. Imagine if adults witnessed the same apparition, they would summon a scientist to carbon date the form!!!!

Perhaps we are now able to fully understand my favorite Beatitude from the New Testament. "Blessed are the pure in heart, for *they* shall see God."

While many may agree that the Divine manifests in the form of various saints and sages, do we even try to *see* these same qualities in each other?

Times of great strife often clearly express our strengths *and* weaknesses. Those thoughts and emotions that were sublimated during calm moments may loom during a crisis. The longer the crisis lasts, the more likelihood for those deep feelings to arise. Often, we hear that traumatic events on a large scale bring out the neighborly side of our personalities. Sometimes it may also cause us to retreat inward, or even resort to actions we might not have taken when all was well. How we react seems to indicate the degree we have incorporated the whispers from our spiritual nature.

In one African nation, a ravaging civil war ripped families apart. Many of the men who fought to defend their homes and freedom never returned to those they attempted to safeguard. Large numbers of women and even children were missing. Feeling the lessening of their small community, the remaining women had to share the often-overwhelming quantity of chores. They toiled in the fields and tended the home, while nurturing and rearing the children. It would have broken a nation with less internal strength, courage, and most of all, faith.

With survival demanding their every waking minute, the future of the country loomed. They were now being advised of the vast number of orphaned children that their country held. What could be done about these children without families? Many were homeless and uncared for, a very dire situation.

Asked for help, the United Nations and a few non-governmental agencies tried to find solutions. The only way, they concluded, was to ask the world at large to adopt these orphaned children. The wheels were set in motion. Kind people from across the globe opened their homes and hearts to these displaced youngsters. The problem was on its way to being solved. Or was it?

As the preparations were being made, a newly formed council of women had great trepidation and doubt. Identifying the needs and the conditions of their country, they realized the great loss of men and women had caused their once sizable population to be greatly reduced. If they sent their most precious resource, the children, from their homeland, their chances of survival as a nation would be in peril. Many had fought against their own brethren for the right to live in a free land; would they now lose all by being overtaken by a foreign government?

Grateful for the generous offers to adopt their precious children, they searched their souls. The message they envisioned heartened them to graciously refuse. The solution rose from the revelation that we are one with everything and everyone. They saw clearly that the children are reflections of the one light in everyone's soul.

With that understanding, the women came up with a practical yet all-encompassing solution. Most of the women holding the burden of running the war-torn country already had multiple children of their own. It was difficult to feed and clothe those they gave birth to. Could they expand their hearts and households to include one or two more children? The answer was a resounding YES!

Over the next few weeks, all the children needing a home and loving family found one. Each woman added one or more grateful children to her household. As her family grew, her initial acceptance of the once-outsider now became love. When we invoke the inner vision and see the same light in all, the idea of a stranger ceases to exist.

Namaste, When I am in the place of love and oneness, I know everything, Namaste.

We cherish the examples in our lives that remind us of the oneness in all. Some of those examples are lesser known, as the brave women in Africa, others are more familiar and inspire us in simple ways, enhancing our lives.

Entering the lobby of a very busy hotel in New Delhi, I had to maneuver my way around a group of men huddled near the door. On closer examination there seemed to be a figure dressed in maroon in the center of the men in suits.

Inching my way through the crowd, I suddenly found myself face to face with His Holiness the Dalai Lama. We seemed to surprise each other.

"Oh, hello," he said, "where are you from?"

"The U.S."

"Come, walk with me." We silently escorted each other to his waiting car. Anticipating the next step, I stood next to His Holiness silently. Thinking what a wonderful memento this memory would make, the idea of a photo wandered into my mind. I tentatively asked permission to take the picture, and he instantly took my hands and held them close to his heart, as an answer. "Take your time," he said to the photographer. Enjoying the close proximity to this holy being, I drifted into a quiet place, observing my consciousness expanding.

After a time, the photos taken, my husband thanked His Holiness. "You have done so much for this world by speaking of the need to remain peaceful and to be kind and loving to one another, we both want to express our gratitude."

Turning to face us directly, he said, "There are almost 8 billion people living on this earth. Why do we not get along? We tend to see people as *other*, rather than seeing them as ourselves. If we could change our attitudes toward each other, we would know they have the same hopes and fears as we do. Peace would prevail."

Later that day, returning from our outing, we spoke to the workers in the hotel about our experience with the

Dalai Lama. From the manager to the cleaning staff, each had a heart-centered comment. The consensus was that he seemed to see everyone as himself, not judging as to job, title, or status. He seemed to live his adage, "My religion is Kindness."

With the revelation of the *Ajna Chakra,* the confusion of duality ends; we navigate the realm of a new reality that catapults us from the world of differences to the reality of *oneness.*

Namaste, When I am in the place of love and oneness, I know everything, Namaste.

Meditation on the Ajna Chakra
• • • • •

Begin by placing a lit candle directly in front of you at eye level.

Allow the body and mind to become quiet.

Feel yourself softening into a deep stillness and peace.

Allow the eyes to close.

Take in a few deep breaths and let them out very slowly.

Bring the awareness to the third eye in the center of the forehead.

There, awaiting your awareness, is a whirling vortex of energy emanating a glowing vibration of violet color.

This vibration generates outward as the *Ajna Chakra*.

It invites us to open to the vastness of universal knowledge.

We then see beyond the earth's qualities. Divine qualities are revealed.

Observe your breath as it flows in and out with ease.(a few moments)

Slowly open the eyes halfway.

Begin to gaze at the light of the candle.

Allow the eyes and eyelids to remain relaxed and soft.

Resist the temptation to reach out and grasp the image with your vision.

Allow the image to flow toward you.

At first, the eyes may wander.

Gently bring them back to the candle flame.

Continue to gaze outward.

The breath remains gentle.

If at any time, you feel the need to blink, or if the eyes tear or feel any discomfort, allow them to gently close.

When ready, softly close the eyes.

With the eyes closed, observe the image of light as seen by the inner vision. (a few moments)

As the inner image begins to fade, allow the eyes to open.

Begin to again gaze toward the external candle light.

After a few minutes allow the eyes to close, drawing deep within.

Clearly "see" the image with the inner eye. (one minute)

Be still as the light enters the eyes and floods your entire being.

If the mind starts to wander or brings in stories about the light, or something totally unrelated, gently bring the awareness back to the candle flame in front of you.

Let all the thoughts and the feelings drift into the background as you contemplate the sacred flame.

Repeat this sequence several times—gazing outward and gazing inward.

When you are able to keep the focus inward, gently allow the eyes to close. (a few minutes)

Follow the light as it goes deeper within, opening to the vastness of universal knowledge.

Feel your entire being illuminated with the knowledge that we are all one in the light.

Experience the universal light expanding as it moves through your body, enlivening each cell.

Observe as your thoughts begin to glow with illumination.

Infused with cosmic light, the emotions embrace their highest form.

Feel the radiance of violet, the color of wisdom and knowledge, radiating a luminosity that infuses your entire being both inward and outward. (a few moments)

Use this moment to shine that divine light of wisdom on a particular situation that may be impacting your life.

Focusing the light on this issue, allow the light to shine a beacon of wisdom, resolving any misunderstanding or hurt. (one minute)

Slowly begin to deepen the breath and feel awareness return to the body, mind, and emotions.

Very gently bring the awareness back to the breath.

Notice how still and calm it has become.

Allow the awareness to return to the *Ajna Chakra*.

Create an affirmation allowing you to stay open to that newly acquainted divine light as it continues to impart the secrets of the universe.

Continue to sit quietly for a few minutes, cherishing the light that radiates outward as the *Ajna Chakra*

With the dawning of the inner sight, we connect to the universal consciousness and experience oneness with all.

● ● ● ● ●

Namaste, When I am in the place of love and oneness, I know everything, Namaste.

Chapter Seven

Sahasara Chakra

When I am in a place of love and oneness

I am one with everything

Oneness

I Am Divine

Floating in the universe, I am infinite. There is no trace of body or mind, just an exquisite sense of being weightless, peaceful, boundless. Without the constraints of time, I am eternal and unchanging.

From some distant location, a sound manifests. It is nondescript, a signal that change is occurring. The time has come for me to return to planet Earth, mission—to take a human birth. Wistfully, I obey fulfilling my *Dharma*, my destiny and righteous path. The process of creating a body to house my spirit has begun.

The subtle being, constructed first, is fashioned from light. The first act of creation manifests a brilliant white opalescence that shines like a thousand suns and becomes our crowning glory. This light is a luminous gateway to the divine consciousness.

The *Sahasara Chakra* grants us access to all the crucial elements needed to create a human being. The entire process of constructing and forming is overseen from the peace of our celestial home. The process is similar to building a physical house. First, specific plans are drawn up, this time with the grand architect of *karma*. The progress is viewed as the foundation is poured, the walls (bones and muscles) are erected, the plumbing (systems of elimination) is installed, the electricity (nervous system) hooked up, and finally, a triumphant sound as the roof is raised. The day draws nearer when the body will be fully formed and ready to be inhabited.

Up until the moment we fully inhabit the body at birth, we are living on a separate planet. This dainty planet is encased in our mother's womb. It is through her body that we receive nourishment and life-giving oxygen. At a predetermined time, our comfort is interrupted by violent contractions. We are guided into a position that propels us head first from our safe, warm environment. With little warning, we are expelled into a world that is cold, bright, noisy, and completely foreign. We slide on to planet Earth—*head first*. At the moment of our first breath, we make a contract with the earth. Each time we inhale, life is affirmed. With each exhalation, we let go of our worldly existence. And so it continues for an indeterminate amount of time. As our *Sahasara Chakra* emerges, it first prompts us to remember that we are essential beings of light, seeking to mesh our divinity with our humanity.

The Sahasara Chakra

The *Sahasara Chakra*, known as the thousand-petal lotus, manifests as the gateway to the cosmic energy source. Granted a human form, cosmic energy enters through the crown of the head while it remains rooted in the heavens, creating the *Sahasara* or *Crown Chakra*.

Entering this chakra seems to be more like a power station rather than a dwelling place. It is here, as spirit, we begin our journey to becoming human and it is through this portal that we reunite with our divinity. For most of our time on earth, we seem unaware of any other existence or purpose.

The flow of energy entering the crown is infinite. It is from here the unbroken stream of universal light begins its descending journey through the spine, pausing at six crucial junctions to create whirling vortexes of energy. The newly formed chakras enable us to survive as well as to thrive on this planet. Reaching its final destination at the root *Muladhara Chakra*, the cosmic energy retreats to the base of the spine where it lies dormant until it ultimately begins its ascension back to the source. It is in the formation of the chakras that the cosmic energy interweaves with the earth energy, bestowing us the designation of human beings. Our journey of life on this planet has begun.

Establishing ourselves in the three Earth Chakras, we become enmeshed in the needs of the body and the physical world; to this extent, most of us forget we are also divine. Aiding our remembrance, the luminescent light of the Crown Chakra is the tractor beam linking us to the universal energy at the source.

The Vedic scriptures introduce us to the concept of the heaven above and the earth below, likening it to an upside-down tree with its roots in the heavens and it branches reaching toward the earth. The upward roots draw cosmic energy to nurture our being, while the downward branches delight the earth by drawing energy from her. It is through this alliance that the opposite energies merge, bestowing our Divinely Human existence on this planet.

To squeeze through the narrow tunnel at birth, our entire skull must remold to fit. To oblige this journey, we are born with a skull that, although considered by the average person to be solid bone, has the ability to compress, allowing the head to squeeze through the slender canal. Even after birth, the energy from our *Crown Chakra* continues to flow freely keeping us connected to the cosmos. At the same time, our existence on earth is solidified.

For many years following our sojourn from birth, there remains a soft spot at the crown of the head. To the early anatomists and physiologists, the crown of the head appeared as a fountain or in Latin, *fontanelle*. It seems they had the ability to see light cascading from the top of the head.

Newborns, even though living on the earth, are more of the other world than here. Hovering our hand over the top of a newborn's soft spot we are able to feel, if not see, light or energy. As the crown slowly, slowly, slowly begins to knit together, some of that otherworldliness fades, along with the knowledge of who we really are.

It is interesting to note how, in many religious traditions, this fontanelle is highlighted. Certain orders of Christian monks shave only the very crown of the head, leaving the remaining hair intact. While in the same tradition, the higher clergy don small caps to shroud the sacred spot.

In both the Muslim and Jewish traditions, skull caps are worn by men in a similar way to the clergy in Christianity, while in the Hindu and Buddhist traditions it is common to see heads completely shaved, allowing the *Sahasara Chakra* to cascade light unencumbered. When a truth is universal, all realize its existence.

The experience of traveling through the tunnel to embrace life, while a difficult journey, is considered a worthy one, as we are then blessed with a human birth. In the annals of time, our life on earth is extremely brief. One scripture describes this brief period of time like a fish living in the sea, leaping as it breaks the surface of the water. Flying through the air for the briefest of moments, it then plunges back to its home in the sea. That blip in time illustrates our fleeting time on earth. How brief our life is, compared to time itself.

Because of its rarified qualities, the *Sahasara Chakra* does not hold many of the earthly attributes that we experienced in the previous chakras. It does not house a sense or an emotion, as it is beyond the earth's jurisdiction and is severed from any of the earthly characteristics. Even the color it radiates is not a color, per se; rather it is the merging of all colors, appearing as white.

As the cosmic light enters the Crown Chakra it takes on an opalescent hue, diffusing into a rainbow of colors, manifesting varied attributes as it enters the other chakras. It is very similar to observing daylight streaming in the window. On first observation, the sunlight looks clear and colorless. To see its diffusion, hang a faceted crystal in the light and marvel at the way the clear light splinters into a rainbow of color. In a similar way, the light from the *Sahasara Chakra* creates prisms, unfurling the spectrum of colors that then imbues the other six chakras. It confirms our broadened knowledge that everything, even color, comes from the one.

The radiant light can be described as opalescent or like a diamond, with multi-facets. The dazzling attribute of a cut diamond comes from two perspectives. It reflects light from within as well as from the outside. The result is that the light diffuses into many facets, causing a kaleidoscope of colors.

The white light radiating from the *Sahasara Chakra* has significance in many cultures. The qualities of purity and spirituality are often linked to the color white. With its lack of other colors causing influence, it is often relegated to those occasions where otherworldliness is called for. Black, being the absence of color and linked to the *Muladhara Chakra*, oversees our basic survival on this earth, while white invokes a transcendental occasion.

It is interesting to note how white and its opposite, black, fare east and west. One of the most obvious ways we recognize the different use of these opposing colors is in the rituals of death. As was mentioned, the portal of the *Sahasara Chakra* ushers us into life, infusing us with the divine essence of universal light and consciousness. When our unrenewable contract expires and our time is near an end, the energy at the base chakra starts to withdraw from the basic survival it has coveted. Slowly beginning its ascension, the energy is withdrawn from the earth. We may feel less like dressing, eating, reading, or wanting new things. A slow, upward meandering detaches us from the worldly pleasures we once cherished. As the energy reaches the crown, the exit is complete.

Many eastern traditions honor this process and rejoice at the soul's liberation from earth's bondage. This holds to their beliefs of reincarnation and rebirth. At the funeral pyre, it is the duty of a Hindu son to break the skull of a parent to allow the spirit to be liberated through the

Sahasara Chakra. All these beliefs are honored through appointing white as the designated color of mourning. The purity of color is a reminder that their loved ones have been released from bodily bondage, free to continue on the soul's journey beyond the earth's grasp.

Many western traditions adhere to the belief that death is final. When severed from our earthly bonds, our bodies are interred, returning earth to earth. As for the soul that inhabited the body, the beliefs vary from ascending to a heavenly place, to not having a clearly defined explanation. For these traditions, donning black, the hue of the *Muladhara Chakra* fits their belief of returning the remains to the earth.

Neither indicates how the heart processes loss of a loved one—that seems to be universal. Our hearts ache as our beliefs seek to soothe and uplift. Our views on life and death influence both how we live *and* how we die.

My first initiation into this aspect of the Eastern philosophy of death, coincided with my initial trip to India. I had been studying the teachings of this ancient culture under the direct tutelage of one of her great masters for many years. The excitement I felt was like a million butterflies invading my whole being.

Arriving very late at night in the capital city of Delhi, the fatigue I accrued from 20-plus hours in the airplane allowed me to sleep for only a few hours, 'til dawn crept in through the curtains. Revealed by the brilliant sunlight, an amazing scene unfolded beneath the balcony. People in simple shelters were going about their morning ablutions at the outdoor facilities. Brushing teeth and washing in plain sight for anyone to see gave me a bit of jolt. Looking around at the apparent luxury of the hotel room I was in, my heart had difficulty reconciling the vast inequality. That is where I wanted to go. I wanted to visit the *real* India, not the four- or five-star variety. Quickly dressing, my roommate and I sought out the dining room for breakfast.

As we approached the breakfast room, the emptiness echoed. Where could everyone be? It was not *that* early. Wandering around the lobby, we found a small group gathering around the teletype machine (way before fax or email). We walked over to see what was so important; the reverent whispers alerted me that something tragic had occurred.

It was revealed to us that Indira Gandhi, prime minister of India, had been shot by her bodyguard and had died from the wounds, less than one mile from our hotel. Shock ricocheted through the building, the city, and the nation.

Yet, being our first time to India, we wanted to explore. Our Guru, knowing India and the way her people react to this type of incident, warned us to stay inside for safety. Our constant persuasion granted us one quick trip out of the hotel. With a wink, my partner and I hopped into an auto rickshaw. "Where to?" the driver asked.

"Please take us to where you live," I said without hesitation. He became silent, unable to understand what we meant. "I want to see where the people of India live, not be sequestered in a fancy hotel."

"You want to see where I live?" Relieved, he finally understood; we both nodded our heads and held on as the rickshaw took off to the place where he lived!

We ground to a stop in front of a large maze of tents and shelters that were originally meant to be temporary, now serving as permanent structures. Leaving us in the vehicle, our guide excused himself but quickly returned with the only other person in the tent city who spoke English. Our gracious host greeted us and motioned to follow him for a "tour."

Proudly, he walked us through the complex, gesturing to the highlights: the medical clinic, houses, bath house, and when finally we found ourselves in the heart of the community, the kitchen. Unlike any kitchen I had known, it seemed efficient for an outdoor cooking arena. Many women were busy preparing enormous amounts of food. "Does the community always prepare such quantities of food?"

"Ah! No, this is a very special occasion. They are preparing a feast!"

Innocently I asked, "What is this special occasion? A wedding, the birth of a baby?"

Shaking his head with a big toothless smile, he expounded, "We are celebrating the death of my brother."

I wanted to clear my ears, as I was sure what I heard could not be correct. "Excuse me, did you say your brother just died?"

"Yes, that is correct. He is now freed from his earthly bondage. We are celebrating."

Feeling a bit humbled, I had read and studied the *Bhagavad Gita*'s teaching that we are all blessed with immortality, but this man was *living it!* The *Gita* to many is a great spiritual text, but to our host, it was his guidebook for living.

For my introduction to India, the spirit of death loomed large. Within these two events, I could see clearly how death is not an outsider but an integral part of their life. Is death something we can all learn to celebrate? Can we focus on the idea that, through death, our loved ones are released from pain, suffering, poverty, oppression? Modern medicine may have the ability to prolong life, but what does that mean for the quality of life? If we welcome the new baby with celebration, why is the other side of the birth-death continuum, not feted as well?

Asked whether she believed in reincarnation, Elisabeth Kübler-Ross, a pioneer in near-death studies replied, "I do not *believe* in reincarnation, I *know* it to be true."

As we begin to fathom the connection between the *Sahasara Chakra* and our divine nature, we are able to comfortably transmit the highest qualities and recognize oneness, once attributed only to saints and sages.

Trying to understand the essence of our divine nature pales as the light of the divine self dawns, unleashing the power of that unfathomable essence. It is only with this realization that we are able to experience everything as being composed of light. Glowing from within, we greet each other's light and we joyfully merge.

Namaste, When I am in the place of love and oneness, I am one with everything, Namaste.

Even as we choose a spiritual teacher or mentor, do we really understand who they are? We measure them against our knowledge of what we think a spiritual teacher should be. Can you imagine a guide who looks like you? Or, do they need to look like something *da Vinci* would paint on the ceiling of a chapel? The holy books say, "We (mortals) are created in the image of the Divine." What are we comparing? Is it the physical form? The color of our skin and hair, gender? If these are our parameters, the choices are definitely narrowed.

Instead, when we gauge our likeness on the presence of the light within, the options for gurus and spiritual teachers becomes infinite. *Sahasara Chakra's* subtle nature—devoid of body, mind, and emotions—functions as a spiritual source rather than an everyday wellspring. When we have mastered the access to this chakra, it becomes a place of refuge where the memory of our soul's divinity is continually recharged, through the essential light.

In the ageless monastic tradition of which I was initiated, the Guru and the Divine are considered to be the same. It was with this understanding that I took final vows. That does not mean, however, that doubts and rebellious actions were absent from my monastic life. Often, when given a task, my mind would question and, often, doubts would come.

There were even times when those reservations grew in gargantuan proportions. One such day I was feeling a bit more frisky than usual. I had been asked to do something that caused great doubts as to the efficacy of the path I was treading. Not wanting to hold this type of mental uncertainty, I decided to have a one-on-one conversation with my Guru. Being that his body was thousands of miles away, a photo would have to do.

Sitting down with the photo, I began to recite my doubts. As I continued to talk to his photo, it became very hazy. I blinked a few times to clear my vision; it remained blurred. My body and mind stilled as the picture continued to fade. After a time, the only thing left in the picture frame was an iridescent, opalescent white glow, without a figure in the center.

Timeless, I drifted out of the body. Without words or thoughts, I realized who my Guru *really* was, not a body in flowing orange robes but a vast ocean of light. Remaining in that place, the realization came that it was not only he who was light, but we were both one in the same light.

Lacking any physical qualities, the *Sahasara Chakra* has many occult and mystical aspects that have long been the subject of religious scriptures. We are told stories of angels, beings of light, appearing to announce great comings and also to warn us of danger. The chosen few who have experienced these beings of light are often heralded as saints or punished as heretics. We even hear tales of these oracles deemed mentally unstable and institutionalized for life. While most endured either great praise or pain, they were all in some way transformed. All lives are changed as the Crown Chakra opens and the cosmic energy flows in, taking various forms, including the recognition that we are beings of light.

Tapping into this mystical chakra, much of what is revealed cannot be rationalized or even justified. Some accounts become fodder for myths and legends. We become enthralled with otherworldly beings in fantasy books or movies. Sitting for hours, wide-eyed, we take in every action that is performed without the confines of a physical body or the earth's gravitational force. Afterward, we try to imagine what it would feel like to fly through the air or gently perch on a shoulder to whisper helpful words. How much reality is woven into these stories is unknown. Where did those ideas come from? Was it merely imagination, or could it be a message from the higher realms, prompting us to leap beyond what we experience with our physical senses? The idea that we are far removed from our spiritual origin remains one of the greatest wonderments.

The ability to activate healing energy is not specific to this chakra. As we discussed in the previous chapters, healing is a gift from *each* chakra. As the power within each chakra is initiated, its own specific attribute for healing is manifested. While the *Anahatha Chakra* may offer healing through touch, prayer would be the healing manifestation of the *Vishudda Chakra*. Being more elusive, the *Sahasara*, unencumbered by physical restrictions is able to expand the previously contained light, for healing. As our consciousness expands, our transcendental skills are honed; we are able to summon and direct this healing light into elusive territory.

While channeling healing energy through touch or prayer is very effective, the *Sahasara* energy, being of a mystical nature, is invoked by means beyond our conscious control. This subtle healing could come as a message through dreams, the result of a traumatic event, or by a prayer of abandonment. When every means has been tried, we reach toward the all-pervading light for solutions or support.

The room, mystically shrouded in candlelight, revealed a cluster of robed monks whispering solemn prayers. The object of the vigil was the lifeless body of a fledgling monk who had recently pledged his now-shortened life to the service of God.

The humble stature of the novice monk did nothing to lessen the outpouring of sincere devotion. The atmosphere, heavily blanketed with prayer, hovered over the bed. Through the mounting dedication of his brethren, the night vigil swept into a crescendo by morning. With the light of a new day, a miracle dawned. The once-lifeless body began to sparkle, emitting light, pulsating with vitality and grace. The soul, burgeoning to another dimension, had returned with renewed vigor to the physical, energetic, and mental-emotional bodies!

Years later, in a magnificent cathedral outside of Paris, I found myself in the presence of this same monk, now considered to be a great healer and holy man. The lavish crowd, buzzing with hope, gathered to witness the miracle of healing. When he returned from the grips of death to the physical world, he found the gift to heal others was his boon. The faithful, being aided by loved ones, arrived by car, van, and private ambulances. The parade of hopefuls was infiltrated by the sorrowful, all arriving for the same purpose—healing. The heartstrings twanged as we witnessed small children in distress, some unable to walk, intermingling with the terminally ill and the elderly.

The healing ceremony began with the celebration of Mass. When the simple monk took his place next to the altar, a tangible hush electrified the room. He began to pray and call out characteristics of the people rather than their names. "Will the small child wearing a red shirt who has been stricken with paralysis, please stand up and walk." To the amazement of those in witness, the child contorted a moment before he straightened, stood up, slid off the gurney, and walked! The next was an elderly terminal cancer patient; on and on it went.

After many hours, people began to feel the mystical cocoon deflate, causing a slow procession toward the exit. The solemn disappointment of those unable to link into the healing light was palpable. Showing great compassion, the monk soothed their doubts and shattered dreams, proclaiming that this healing was not possible for everyone, as it was dependent on what fate had in store for them. For many of us present, the fallout from the direct healing and ritual sparked our inner spiritual light.

The example above is considered by many an acceptable way to focus healing light. For generations, we have sought out clergy, mystical or not, as healers. They offer prayers and rituals, while those with gifts may use touch or focus the light for healing.

Namaste, When I am in the place of love and oneness, I am one with everything, Namaste.

The word *healing* has been relegated to the religious while the act of *curing* was the domain of the medical community. Some modern medical wonders seem very mystical. Even the simple act of taking an aspirin or analgesic for pain can seem otherworldly. As a child, I tried to grasp the concept of how a small unmarked pill would know exactly where my pain was. By swallowing it, the pain would vanish. This was beyond what my young mind could fathom. Questioning my patient mother before ingesting the tablet, "How does it know where to go? What if it goes to my toe instead of my headache?" Persuading me to accept the remedy, she answered, "I wrote a note on the pill telling it where to go!" Satisfied with that logic, I swallowed the remedy and, like magic, the headache disappeared. We chuckle that this is the innocence of a child's mind, yet many of our modern drugs seem to have a magical tint to them.

What happens if the mystical and the medical model collide? Can we, with the more scientific leaning, accept that at a certain time the two merge? The medical certainties of the modern age, if performed hundreds of years ago, would be major miracles. The idea of taking out a damaged organ or joint and replacing them with another has kept science fiction engaged for decades. What is now becoming commonplace in modern medicine will be obsolete in the not too distant future.

What remains a constant is the body and mind's ability to heal and accept treatments that would otherwise be detrimental. These treatments not only prolong lives but enhance them. Many of us know people whose quality of life has been greatly limited because of hip or knee issues. Thanks to modern medicine, an artificial part is popped in; dancing is now in their repertoire. Looking at a pig, who could have predicted that its heart valve could be used to restore an ailing human heart to a healthy beat?

For those skeptical of anything unscientific, the mystical can slip in with no logical explanation to convince even the cynics that miracles happen every day. This is a story about a doctor friend of mine who, before this incident, called anything mystical *woo-woo!*

The moment anticipated for the past nine months had arrived. With the gushing of liquid, Jean carefully went over the rehearsed checklist. Gather the packed suitcase from the closet, *check*. Call the cat sitter, *check*, Call the doctor, *check*, Call husband to meet me at the hospital, *check*.

All in order, she slowly walked to the waiting car and driver. She had planned well and was now off to deliver her precious baby. Between contractions on the drive to the hospital, she was able to contact her husband with the joyous news, and was rewarded with the assurance that he was on his way and would meet her at the hospital.

Arriving at the hospital, Jean was whisked into Labor and Delivery with only moments to spare. Or, so they thought. Those moments, without warning, turned into a looming nightmare. The infant's heart was showing signs of distress. If it did not right itself soon, a surgical procedure would become the savior of this small infant. Reluctant to do anything radical without the emotional support of her husband, Jean begged for a few more minutes. Certain he would arrive momentarily, mother and baby were closely monitored.

As he hastened out of the office, Jack's knowing colleagues gave a cheer for good luck. Taking the most direct route to the hospital, he was on his way to comfort his beloved and to greet their soon-to-be-born child.

Fate had a different agenda. With a sudden and severe pain gripping his chest, Jack fell unconscious and the car, now devoid of a driver, crashed into the median strip. Unaware of the chaotic scene around him, Jack floated peacefully in another realm. The rescuing ambulance sped through traffic with sirens ablaze, ultimately arriving at the ER of the very same hospital where his wife was laboring. Like lightning, the experienced medical team began life saving maneuvers and connected Jack to monitors and machines. Yet, with all modern medical marvels, both Jack and his baby remained in critical condition.

Hearing a loud beeping sound, Jean realized that waiting for her husband was no longer an option if the baby was to survive. She reluctantly gave her approval for surgery to commence.

The same warning beep was now present for Jack in the trauma room, as the monitors showed no heart activity. With practiced skill, after what seemed like an eternity, Jack was resuscitated and, while weak, was back among the living.

The good news in the operating room found a successful delivery of a sweet baby boy. Jean's joy was clouded by worry, what could be detaining her husband?

When Jack was stable and in recovery, Jean was told what happened. Grateful for the positive outcome, she was overwhelmed with both fear *and* joy.

When the cardiologist came to check on Jack, his medical experience had not prepared him for what he was being told. After having a heart attack, car crash, and subsequent flat-lining, which rendered him unconscious, Jack had a "dream." He was floating in an etheric environment, surrounded by a sense of peace and tranquility, a state of being previously unknown to him. Feeling as though he wanted to be there always, his bliss was interrupted by another luminous being. Offering good wishes, the being identified himself as Jack's unborn son.

"How could that be?" Jack wondered and asked. "Why are you here?"

"My heart stopped, as did yours, and we were both propelled to this level as a waypoint before merging into the light."

"No, this cannot be possible. You mother will be devastated, you have to go back and live a long life."

"I am not going back without you. I want a complete family, both mother and father to guide and love me."

The wordless discussion continued, with neither moving from their point of view.

Finally the infant suggested, "If we are not going back, then let's continue our journey to the light."

"I cannot be the cause of creating enormous sorrow for my beloved wife; she is kind and loving. This will destroy her." Holding his son's and wife's wellbeing above his own desire to stay in this sublime place, he agreed to return to his body, and life. The promise made, both father and baby at the same moment traversed the void and slipped back into their respective bodies. Instantaneously, the heart monitors which showed cessation of heart activity just moments before, now registered signs of life.

The cardiologist listening to the "dream" had an inkling that it was more than that. Deciding to review the monitors and times of the apparent heart stoppage for both, he was dumbfounded. The monitors revealed the father's heart *and* the baby's heart had ceased beating at the exact same moment. And, as incredible as it may sound, both hearts recommenced simultaneously.

Could the father's "dream" have been a mystical meeting with his unborn child? His telling left some wondering what all this could mean. Others chalked it up to hallucinations. But while there was not a consensus among the medical community, there were a few mavericks who reached beyond their logical minds to agree—it could have been a transcendental experience! A mystical *and* a medical miracle, at once!

*Namaste, When I am in the place of love and oneness,
I am one with everything, Namaste.*

The more these stories are told, the more commonplace and accepted they become. Many of us have had some kind of mystical experience in our lifetime. Perhaps as a child, a being of light was present. It might have even become your pal, someone to talk to. Sometimes in our darkest time we call out and are rewarded with an answer. When the dialog begins and people share these experiences, it opens the portal for those a bit shyer to share.

Once there has been a personal experience with a being

The Namaste Effect

of light, doubt flies away. It is our distrust and questioning that keep portals closed. With this closure, our only option is to remain confined to the cognitive mind as our main source of information. If we allow our mystical awareness to expand, situations we have not yet begun to imagine, manifest. With that comes the acknowledgement that we are multi-faceted beings with hidden mysteries, most of which we are yet unable to fully grasp. When we are courageous enough to take the leap of faith and embrace the gifts the Heaven Chakras can offer, the rewards are multifold.

Sharon and her sweetie were walking back after a rejuvenating yoga class. Holding his hand, she felt a deep unease from her partner. He seemed unable to express his discomfort, and they silently walked to the subway. As they climbed down the multiple layers to the inner tunnel at the station, the unease became a nervous anxiety. Along with a few people, they awaited the train's arrival.

Seeing the bright light lumbering on the tracks, there was a bit of relief flooding Sharon's body. Moving toward the edge of the platform anticipating the arrival, she felt a strong shove as her body went airborne from the platform to land splayed directly on the tracks of the oncoming train. Shock ricocheting through her body and mind, she was unable to move or think. Fearing the end of her young life was near, her prayers flew wordlessly, reaching beyond all comprehension.

As time slowed, she could hear the approaching train nipping at her toes. Amongst all the mechanical sounds, she began to hear angelic voices. "Let's pick her up and move her to the middle of the tracks. Unable to believe her ears, she opened her eyes and followed her prayers to a mystical place of love and light. There she saw four luminous beings of an opalescent white. They did not acknowledge her gaze, as they were busy accomplishing their immediate mission.

Task completed, they pivoted their compassion to her fear and emotions. "We are here to protect you, have no fear. Your body is now safe and after the train passes all will be well." As they spoke, Sharon felt her being become light. She watched with dispassionate interest as the underside of the train rolled along the tracks above her well-protected body.

The luminescent beings of light stayed with her through the rescue and voyage to the hospital. They became her ever-present angels during her recovery. With all the trauma she had been through, her body had survived and was intact except for an injury to her foot, an injury that at first she feared would prevent her from the joy of her life, dancing. With her renewed courage and light "friends," her recovery progressed with ease. And her dancing? She is able to abandon herself to the movements with ease and grace, almost as if she is being held up by angels.

Namaste, When I am in the place of love and oneness, I am one with everything, Namaste.

For millennia, we have sought advice from the scriptures to help us venture into the worlds beyond what the eyes can see, the ears can hear, or any other external way to discern reality. This seems to be universal among different traditions. The appearance of celestial beings in holy books inspires the possibility of their presence.

Some of the important passages reveal hope of an upcoming invitation to the hidden realms, deemed accessible to only a few. The difficulty seems to be in the ability to adequately explain a concept that is beyond words.

After the theater in New York City, we joined our friends in the hotel lobby to decide on dinner plans. Happy to be together, we played catch-up on our lives since last we met. At a certain moment in the visit, I became restless and dizzy. Fearing I would fall into a swoon, I excused myself to douse my face with water. Reaching the hotel room, I had to sit down on the bed and take deep breaths. Still feeling somewhat out of my body, I revived sufficiently and rejoined my friends.

We had a delicious dinner and visit, making sleep a welcome visitor that night. An early morning phone call validated the physical concerns from the night before. It seems that my Guru Swami Satchidanandaji had, while in India, left his body the night before. Could it have been at the time the dizziness occurred?

Quickly rearranging my plans, I joined my spiritual family at the ashram for both solace and remembering. Since he died in India, the body had to be transported to the U.S., where it would be retrieved at the closest point of entry. Awaiting the arrival of the body, the senior disciples gathered, bringing comfort and consolation to each other. Upon the arrival of his earthly remains, one of my dear friends, experiencing trepidation, asked me to join her in viewing the body of our beloved teacher. Being the only ones present, we entered his resting place in hushed tones. An eerie sensation filled the room. With humble respect, we approached the coffin. Holding her hand, I peeked in, acknowledging the form I had pledged my love and devotion to for many years.

Suddenly I heard my Guru's voice. More than a bit shocked, I instinctively looked around. "Why are you looking for me in the box. I am not in there. You are looking for the form that *was* me. I am now light, as you are also."

Shocked and a bit intimidated by the disembodied voice, I turned to the only other living person in the room. "Did you hear that?" I asked. No. I shared what message I had received. Not missing a beat, we held hands as joy coursed through our being, causing us to start dancing. Our Guru had given us a parting gift, reminding us that we are made up of pure light. Something to rejoice about when we leave the physical body. All that we are merges with the divine light and that light is the same light in all.

> "I wish I could show you, when you are lonely or in darkness, The Astonishing Light of Your Own Being." —Hafiz

Namaste, When I am in the place of love and oneness, I am one with everything, Namaste.

Meditation on the Sahasara Chakra

● ● ● ● ●

Allow the body and mind to become quiet.

Feel yourself softening into a deep stillness and peace.

Allow the eyes to close.

Take in a few deep breaths and let them out very slowly.

Bring the awareness to the thousand petal Lotus at the crown of the head.

There, awaiting your awareness, is a whirling vortex of energy emanating a glowing vibration of opalescent white.

This vibration generates outward as the *Sahasara Chakra*.

It is a portal into the vastness of the universe where we see beyond the earth's qualities to reveal divine qualities.

Observe your breath as it flows in and out with ease. (one minute)

Slowly begin to focus on the light emanating from the crown of your head.

With the inner vision, notice how the light transforms the top of your head to light.

Notice how the light streams in from a distant source. (a few moments)

With the next inhalation, direct the light as it floods your entire body.

Taking in a deep breath, notice how the light brightens.

With the exhale send that light out to the world.

Inhale and direct that light to touch all the internal organs and every cell in your body.

Your whole-body fills with light. (a few moments)

Allow that light to expand past the periphery of the physical body.

Inhale, the light brightens.

Exhale, send light out to the world as love.

Continue to expand the light until it fills the entire room.

Inhale, the light brightens. Exhale, send that light out to the world as love. (a few moments)

Allow the light to expand beyond the room to fill the entire dwelling with light.

Inhale, the light brightens. Exhale, send that light out to the world as love. (a few moments)

Continue to follow the light as it moves out through the windows and doors, flowing down the streets and walkways, touching every living thing with light and love.

Allow it to continue to flow into the streams and rivers meeting the ocean.

As you inhale, the light brightens.

Exhale, send that light and love out to the world, passing over towns and cities, countries and continents.

Inhale, the light brightens. Exhale, send that light and love out to the world.

Allow this divine light to form a circle of light surrounding the entire earth, allowing all to experience the light of their own true self.

Continue to inhale as the light brightens, and with the exhale send light and love out to the world. (one minute)

Slowly allow the light to return and enter through the top of the head.

Feel your entire being illuminated with the one light.

Experience the radiant opalescent white light infusing your entire being, both inward and outward. (a few moments)

Slowly begin to deepen the breath as you feel the awareness return to the body and the breath.

Notice how still and calm the breath has become.

Create an affirmation that summons the secrets of the universe revealed through the universal light.

Affirm that the same light that shines within us, shines in all. We are one in the light.

Continue to sit quietly for a few minutes welcoming

the resplendent light that radiates as the *Sahasara Chakra*.

Through that light, we connect to the universal consciousness and experience oneness with all.

● ● ● ● ●

Namaste, When I am in the place of love and oneness, I am one with everything, Namaste.

The Namaste Effect

Continuing Namaste

*Namaste,
When I am in the place of Love and Oneness
and you are in the place of Love and Oneness,
We are One, Namaste.*

The Namaste Effect came into being with the intention to shed light and understanding on two distinct aspects of our mystical selves. The first being the chakras; while foreign to most, they are one of the most influential of all the subtle aspects that govern our every thought, word and action.

Then there is the sublime and coveted entity we call Love. It is a universal concept which is exhibited in all walks of life, even though most are hard-pressed to define its vastness and noble qualities.

The ominous quality of each of these precepts has the ability to affect both the mundane, as well as the more rarified spiritual realms. If we agree that these perceptions foster daily functions, why then would they be so difficult to discern?

My intention and hope in writing this was to give those who have had a glimpse, or even accumulated intellectual knowledge, a way to place those elusive experiences in their lives. In the case of Love, we may experience some of the intimate aspects, but through the telling of examples and stories, we are able to expand this precious gift beyond our normal circle and limits.

As a small child, I would frequently enter into a semi-trance state and find myself, on the return, seeing colors and feeling love for all. My sweet mother would even comment, "You cannot love everyone!" and my innocent reply was, "Why not?" My experience could not be expressed through any normal rationalization. As much as I asked and searched sources, I was unable to define the vastness of what I was feeling. When I revealed that I was able to see color surrounding an object or person, the condescending smiles would relegate the experience to a child's imagination.

It was not until many years later I discovered insights into these unusual behaviors by piecing together information from books and spiritual teachers. Although the word *love* is well used, or some say overused, it stays in its limitations, as we tend to think of loving as a personal affair. This makes it difficult to find a fit for the feelings of love we might experience for the earth or for those we have yet to meet.

Our journey through the chakras presents *love* as multifaceted, expanded, unlimited, and wholehearted. It is offered in an expansive way that seems to be opposite to the way it is often portrayed, which is less indicative of its luminous expression. If we are able to express love within a certain comfort level, needing to compress and categorize it in order to contain its vastness, it is deemed manageable. It might become controllable, but is that the best venue for its expression? In this way, we may understand love, but love at its core is beyond understanding. It must be set free to roam and merge with what appears in its path. It is then that we can allow it to expand further than our minds can comprehend.

My hope is that you were able to identify with some of the protagonists in the many stories offered. They were intended to inspire, heal wounds, and offer possible solutions to life's continuing challenges.

If the *Namaste Effect* inspired you, continue to delve deeper into the study of the chakras, from an experiential and mystical aspect as well as well-grounded explanations. We are fortunate in these times to have a wide range of books, DVDs, or online classes that inspire us to explore the chakras. Of course, nothing replaces the direct and personal experience of an informed teacher.

As a very effective means of exploration, as mentioned

in *The Namaste Effect*, begin to cultivate a spiritual practice or enhance an already established practice with some of the meditations offered. Become aware of any messages or attributes that are derived directly from a particular chakra. Allow the knowledge gained to ascertain the chakra at its origin. The more awareness placed on the chakras as a whole, or on particular chakras, the more they reveal their inner workings.

With the aspect of Universal Love, our emphasis is less on understanding the concept, rather focusing on its ability to expand the heart so we are able to love unconditionally, without hesitation.

To fully embrace the chakras from an intuitive prospective, cultivate a depth of understanding and integration in your daily life. One fun way to do this is to emphasize one chakra each day of the week. Coincidentally, there are Seven Mystical Chakras *and* seven days of the week. This makes it easy to embrace one chakra each day.

Begin at the base, by dedicating an entire day to the *Muladhara Chakra*. Wear the color and choose a practice that expresses Universal Love in that chakra. For example, awakening in the morning, choose to follow the attributes of the Earth's vibration. Since the earth surrounds us and our bodies are made from it, the immediate aspect we might choose to express is gratitude for the earth's support in our basic survival. Choose the color red as an article of clothing, a red placemat for breakfast, or a bouquet of red carnations placed on your work desk. The external color vibration will call out the red hue from the chakra, and the attributes will become available to you.

Continuing to honor the earth's vibration in the *Muladhara Chakra*, choose to bathe in warm water laced with mineral salts as a service to yourself. For broader service to others, visit a homeless shelter, volunteering to serve food for a few hours. Take notes on what you did and how the actions made you feel.

As the next day dawns, choose another chakra and continue with your exploration. It is helpful to visit the chakras in order, but if one calls to you, trade order for spontaneity.

It would be ideal to match the chakras with the planets that govern the days of the week. From ancient times, the days of the week were given names based on the planets that influence them. Sunday is the day of the sun, as Monday is the day of the moon. However, determining which of the planets govern each of the chakras is still unclear. Some say Monday, Moon Day, governs the *Swadhisthana Chakra*, as it is concerned directly with emotion. Others say it is Venus. If you have an intuitive feeling for a particular chakra on a given day, go with that inspiration. It is wise to create a simple ritual rather than complicating it by matching it to the planets. If you like clear systems and routine, choose any day of the week to start (often, Sunday works best, as many consider it the first day of the week). Begin with the *Muladhara Earth Chakra* and then on Monday choose the *Swadhisthana* and continue. That way it will be clear exactly which chakra to honor on a given day.

If you are more free flowing, as you awaken choose the color and chakra that vibrates with you on that day. Be sure to include every chakra within the week. With this more random method, copious notes are necessary. Journaling becomes an important aspect for either mode, as it allows us to see which chakra and part of our lives we need to place more emphasis on, and which are more in balance.

The greater our focus, the deeper our experience of the chakras becomes. By allowing the intuitive to reveal the deepest understanding of the chakras, our lives become adaptable to changes and open to infinite possibilities.

Make the knowledge of the Mystical Chakras your constant companion at every turn and action by becoming intimately acquainted with each of the chakras and their qualities. This allows us to touch the depth of our divine essence.

Live your fullest potential by tapping into the greatest source of wisdom in the entire universe.

Embrace the concept of Universal Love as your soul's food, satiating your eternal hunger for communion with others.

Place your heart's expression of Love front and center as you embrace all as yourself—*becoming one with everything!*

Namaste

"I honor the place within you where the
entire Universe resides;
I honor the place within you of love, of light,
of truth, of peace;
I honor the place within you, where,
when you are in that place in you,
and I am in that place in me,
there is only one of us."
—Mahatma Gandhi

A Grateful Namaste

Often I am asked why I enjoy watching award shows. Is it for the glamour? The movie stars? The fashions? The entertainment? My answer is yes, all of that. However, one of the main reasons I watch is to bask in the joy of the winners. After the shock of hearing their name called, they begin honoring the people who made their extraordinary performance possible. Almost as if there is an invisible iceberg, the star being at the pinnacle, ninety percent of the work done is unseen. The star's open heart acknowledges the many people who contributed to the show, movie, or song's award-winning success.

Writing a book can have a similar feeling. When the incredible moment finally comes that the author holds the precious tome in their hands, it is their academy award. Most readers engrossed in the story are usually unaware of the amount of imagination, thought, feeling, and true grit, that goes into the final product. The huge number of details called production would no doubt take away some of the magic that happens when we immerse ourselves in a good book.

This book is not an exception to this. Yes, my name is on the cover and I get much of the accolades, and sometimes criticisms, yet how many unseen sources have labored in love to bring it to fruition?

I would like to offer my humble gratitude and a heartfelt Namaste to all who have made this offering possible.

To my spiritual teachers, who have helped me see beyond the physical to a place I yearned for but could not find the right entrance. They acted like a road map, showing me the way. When I would ask Sri Swami Satchidanandaji to help me understand the chakras, he would quietly draw within and encourage me to do the same. "We cannot understand the subtle with the mind, only with the heart. Go within." And so I did. I have been blessed with many great teachers to show me the pathway to my higher self; they all taught love as the highest route. Some of these spiritual teachers were disguised as students and "everyday people" sharing insights and visions.

After publishing two other books and numerous articles and audio works, I appreciate the role of the editor and publisher. I have worked with many who have been extraordinarily helpful in making the finished project smoother and more comprehensible. Some of them were easy to work with. Some were not. Sometimes a friendship emerged. Often when opinions clashed, I had to stand strong to keep my vision of the book intact.

Publishing *The Namaste Effect* brought me the dream team, a true gift in the form of Connie Shelton, a world-renowned mystery writer in her own right and founder/senior partner of Columbine Publishing Group and Lotus Flower Books. She escorted me through the entire process with skill and competence. The planning meetings were smooth and actually fun. Even when we delved into the nitty-gritty details, we traversed them like two friends chatting and creating. This made the whole process easeful, allowing me to feel empowered throughout.

We have all heard the expression "two heads are better than one," and my team has not just brilliant heads but open and compassionate hearts. In this case, the two hearts working together were a dynamic duo. At my first meeting with Stephanie Dewey, I knew we had a winning team.

Soft spoken and extremely competent, she brought in a fresh perspective and numerous skills that rounded out the team. Her positive response to the book bolstered my confidence.

It is always helpful to have friends who are also authors, to create *Satsang*, a support team. Sometimes while talking with my author friends, some already published some about to publish, it was reminiscent of a group of mothers trying to make sense of their children's behavior, which was best done by speaking to someone going through it. Seems I spent many hours on the phone commiserating and marveling at the change in the publishing industry. They were a perfect sounding board, and for this I am grateful.

The task of getting the word out about the book was through the dedicated service from the heart of Kori Gibson. Her aptitude for knowing how to excite people on social media was accompanied by her cheerful nature and enthusiasm, making the project feel like a grand expedition.

In remembrance of my former agent, Loretta Barrett who, 10 years ago, encouraged me to write *The Namaste Effect*. "Love that title!" Sorry, Loretta, it took so long and hopefully you are enjoying it from up in the clouds.

I am grateful to the very busy Yoginis, who took the time out of their full and dedicated service to read the manuscript and write endorsements, sisters in the spirit indeed.

To the love of my life, my partner, Bhaskar, who supports me in who I am, not only in what I do. His dedication and love allow me to venture to places I have never gone before.

Many of the stories included in *The Namaste Effect*, are from friends and students who, with an open heart and sparkling eyes filled with awe, shared their personal miracles or those of a friend. Your stories inspired me and through the sharing I pray that they were well represented, and the essential emotion was captured as well as the lessons learned. If there were mistakes or misrepresentations please know it was unintentional. These heartfelt stories allow us to better understand *our* life and *its* lessons. And my hope is that you will continue to share other heartfelt experiences with me.

To all those who are not mentioned by name, but nonetheless encouraged me in some way, I humbly thank you for all your faith in me and this project. You all hold special places in my heart *and* life.

Much gratitude to you, dear readers and aspirants who hold a keen desire to learn more about the Sacred Chakras system. My hope is that you are inspired, and your hearts are open to embracing Universal Love. As you share what you've learned and experienced, *The Namaste Effect* will spread to all parts of this earth and beyond, uniting every living plant, animal, and person in the entire universe.

To each of you I offer deep bow and a heartfelt
Namaste.

About the Author

NISCHALA JOY DEVI is a masterful teacher and healer. For many years she has been highly respected as an international advocate for her innovative way of expressing Yoga and its subtle uses for spiritual growth and complete healing. Her dynamic delivery and deep inner conviction empower each individual, allowing the teachings to expand beyond boundaries and limitations of any one tradition, enabling her to touch people's hearts.

She was graced to spend many years as a monastic disciple with the world renowned Yogiraj Sri Swami Satchidanandaji, receiving his direct guidance and teachings. She also was blessed with teachings from great Yoga masters in the US, India, and worldwide.

Originally trained in western medicine, she began to blend western medicine with Yoga, offered her expertise in developing the yoga portion of The Dean Ornish Program for Reversing Heart Disease, and co-founded the award-winning Commonweal Cancer Help Program. Her book, *The Healing Path of Yoga*, expresses these teachings.

With her knowledge of Yoga and her experience in assisting those with life-threatening diseases, she created Yoga of the Heart, a training and certification program for Yoga teachers and health professionals, designed to adapt Yoga practices to the special needs of that population.

She is dedicated to bringing the Feminine back into spirituality and the scriptures in her book, *The Secret Power of Yoga, A Woman's Guide to the Heart and Spirit of the Yoga Sutras* and the *Secret Power of Yoga* audio book (Nautilus Book Award Winner).

Understanding the need for more love and compassion

in today's world, *The Namaste Effect*, her most recent book, explores a heart-centered way of living through the mystical chakras.

When not traveling and teaching, she lives with her husband in Arizona and Virginia.

**For information about programs, trainings, and retreats, please visit her website:
www.abundantwellbeing.com**

Printed in Great Britain
by Amazon